Placed
in His Glory

Placed
in His Glory

Fuchsia Pickett

Charisma®
HOUSE

PLACED IN HIS GLORY by Fuchsia Pickett
Published by Charisma House
A part of Strang Communications Company
600 Rinehart Road
Lake Mary, Florida 32746
www.charismahouse.com

Unless otherwise noted, all Scripture quotations are from the New King James Version of the Bible. Copyright © 1979, 1980, 1982 by Thomas Nelson, Inc., publishers. Used by permission.

Scripture quotations marked KJV are from the King James Version of the Bible.

Scripture quotations marked NAS are from the New American Standard Bible. Copyright © 1960, 1962, 1963, 1968, 1971, 1972, 1973, 1975, 1977 by the Lockman Foundation. Used by permission. (www.Lockman.org)

Scripture quotations marked NIV are from the Holy Bible, New International Version. Copyright © 1973, 1978, 1984, International Bible Society. Used by permission.

Scripture quotations marked RSV are from the Revised Standard Version of the Bible. Copyright © 1946, 1952, 1971 by the Division of Christian Education of the National Council of the Churches of Christ in the USA. Used by permission.

Library of Congress Catalog Card Number: 2001087159
International Standard Book Number: 0-88419-752-2

01 02 03 04 05   8 7 6 5 4 3 2 1
Printed in the United States of America

Dedicated to
Stephen and Joy Strang,
two dear friends who have encouraged,
inspired and challenged me to preach
and write the revelation of God's Word
as the Holy Spirit taught me.

And to Dr. Sue Curran, my pastor and friend,
whose life is an open book showing
forth His glory.

IN MEMORY OF

Helen Vincent Washburn
(1906–1945)

Dean of John Wesley Bible College
and Martinsville, VA Bible College.

Known as a "Scripture mystic,"
she was my greatest inspiration as a young Bible
student to know God and His Word.

Contents

Chapter 1

What Is the Glory?

Discerning God's Heart

O ne early Sunday morning I cried out to God as I paced back and forth in front at the altar of my church's sanctuary. With a heavy heart I wept, asking God to send His glory to my church. "Please send Your glory to us," I pleaded.

That was when the Holy Spirit spoke these words to me: "Fuchsia, what are you looking for?"

I responded emphatically, "The glory."

The Holy Spirit is so cute; He can be facetious at times. He continued, "When the glory comes, what will it look like?"

I answered sheepishly, "I don't know."

Then He asked, "What color will it be?"

Still weeping I said, "I don't know."

He persisted, "What shape will it be?"

Feeling almost embarrassed then, I had to respond once more, "I don't know."

Then He said, "If you don't know what the glory looks like, what color or shape it is, how will you know when it gets here?"

I didn't know how to respond to that question, but His communication was clear.

That was the last word the Holy Spirit spoke to me that morning and for several weeks after that. He didn't explain to me how to recognize the glory. He was silent, and my heart remained heavy, wondering if our church would ever enjoy the glory of God, though I wasn't at all sure what that would mean. I had graduated from seminary with an earned doctorate in theology, had pastored many years and taught seminary classes. Yet I did not know how to define the glory of God that I was so desperate for my church to experience. Dumb? Yes! I simply didn't know what to expect.

We have heard for years that the glory is coming. We sing songs about God sending us His glory. But, from where? And how will we know when it is here?

2

A few weeks later I was standing on the platform one Sunday morning during a very intense worship service, singing songs of high praise and enjoying the presence of the Lord. I had my hands raised and my eyes closed, praising God, when "Someone" punched me. I had felt that punch before, so I knew it was the Holy Spirit getting my attention. "Open your eyes," He commanded.

We had a large group of young people in our church, so I thought that He was calling my attention to them to see which one of them was misbehaving. I looked in their direction to see whom I needed to correct, but they were all worshiping. I looked around and didn't see anything amiss, so I closed my eyes and went back to worshiping.

A few minutes later He punched me again and told me to open my eyes. I obeyed, but I couldn't see anything except people absorbed in praise and enjoying the presence of the Lord.

I closed my eyes again and felt a third punch. At that moment I knew He meant business. I opened my eyes and heard Him say, "Look at your people." I looked at them and realized they had front porch lights on—their faces were glowing with the glory of the Lord. There was a divine light in the "house," and it was reflecting in their faces. The Holy Spirit used that moment to teach how to recognize the glory of God. At the same time, He answered the anguish of my heart to see the glory of God in my church.

> We have heard for years that the glory is coming. But, from where? And how will we know when it is here?

Of course, there is much more to understanding the glory of God than recognizing His wonderful presence in a worship service. As I have searched the Scriptures concerning the glory of God, I have taken a fascinating journey into the presence of God. Passages of scripture have leaped off the pages with fresh understanding of who God is and how precious humanity is in His great heart of love.

We get a glimpse of the power of God working in every believer's life when Paul declares, "Christ in you, the hope of glory" (Col. 1:27). When Jesus prayed, "Father, I desire that they also whom You gave Me may be with Me where I am, that they may behold My glory," volumes of wondrous truth regarding eternity were revealed (John 17:24). Throughout the Old and New Testaments God reveals His glory to mankind. He desires that born-again believers reflect His glory in the earth. We will do that more perfectly as we allow the Holy Spirit to enlarge our understanding of the glory of God.

DEFINING THE GLORY

Let's begin with a working definition for *the glory of God* taken from *Nelson's Illustrated Bible Dictionary. Glory* refers to a quality of God's character that emphasizes His greatness and authority and involves beauty, power and honor. It is used in three senses in the Bible. First, it may refer to God's moral beauty and perfection of character that is beyond man's understanding. The Scriptures declare that all men fall short of the glory of God (Rom. 3:23).[1]

Glory may refer to God's moral beauty and perfection as a *visible presence.* While God's glory is not a substance, at times God does reveal His perfection to man in a visible way. Such a display of the presence of God is often seen as fire or dazzling light, but sometimes as an act of power. Some examples from the Old Testament include:

 The pillar of cloud and fire—Exodus 13:21

 The Lord's deliverance of the Israelites at the Red Sea—Exodus 14

4

🐾 His glory in the tabernacle—Leviticus 9:23–24

🐾 Solomon's temple—1 Kings 8:11

Since the close of the Old Testament, the glory of God has been shown most completely in Christ (Luke 9:29–32; John 2:11) and in the members of His church. Christ now shares His divine glory with His followers (John 17:5–6, 22), so that in their lives Christians are being transformed into the glorious image of God (2 Cor. 3:18). Believers will be fully glorified at the end of time in God's heavenly presence (Rom. 5:2; Col. 3:4). There, the glory of God will be seen everywhere (Rev. 21:23).

Glory in the Scriptures also refers to the praise and honor that God's creatures give to Him. In this sense we hear the psalmist cry out, "Not unto us, O LORD, not unto us, but to Your name give glory, because of Your mercy, because of Your truth" (Ps. 115:1). To summarize this biblical definition of the glory of God, we can say it refers to:

5

🐾 God's moral beauty and perfection of character

🐾 God's moral beauty as a visible presence

🐾 Praise and honor that God's creatures give to Him

We are hearing so much about the glory in the church these days. It is vital for every sincere believer to grasp the significance of what the glory of God is. If we do not, we will cheapen and lessen the impact of the message the Holy Spirit is speaking to the church today. Being filled with the glory of God is the priority of the Holy Spirit's work in the church corporately—and in our lives individually. According to Jesus' high priestly prayer, it is the glory of God reflected in our lives that will bring the lost to Him. (See John 17.)

> *Glory* refers to a quality of God's character that emphasizes His greatness and authority and involves beauty, power and honor.

As we focus our attention on the biblical pattern for the revelation of the glory of God, we can learn, first of all, where we are falling short of His glory (Rom. 3:23). Then we can position ourselves so that we are being changed into His image, "from glory to glory" (2 Cor. 3:18). As we become divine *glory-bearers,* we will be a part of the great End-Time revival and ingathering of souls that God will bring to those who are seeking His glory. For that to happen, we need to be cleansed of all that hinders us from bearing the glory of God for all to see. To that end, we will discuss many aspects of the scriptural revelation of the glory of God. We will discover how we can more perfectly relate to Him and reflect His glory in the earth.

DIVINE CHARACTER IN TYPE

The first part of our working definition of the glory of God deals with the moral beauty and perfection of the character of God. Because of sin, it is impossible for us to relate to such divine perfection—or even to understand what it is. Our idea of

6

love, for example, is so warped that when the scriptures declare that God is love (1 John 4:7), we must refer to many other verses to describe what God's love looks like, feels like and how it functions.

Since the beginning of time after the fall of mankind, God has been trying to reveal Himself and His glory to His fallen creatures. Such is His desire for a family, for children in His image, that He has gone to extravagant lengths to reveal His love and to tell us what He is like. He has used every conceivable picture—we call them *types, shadows, metaphors, parables*—to help us "see" and understand divinity, that we might be partakers of His divine nature (2 Pet. 1:4).

A *type* prefigures or symbolizes something or someone. It is a person, place, thing, event or incident that is recorded in the Bible to teach us spiritual truths about God or His people. These persons and places were not mythical; they were actual historical facts. The typical events recorded in the Scriptures really happened; they are not mere allegories. But they each convey a truth in type that is larger than the natural realities they represent.

We should always be careful not to set forth anything as a type that the Scriptures themselves do not so designate. But if we dig deeply enough, we shall find that almost every incident in Old Testament history that is referred to in the New Testament has been "typical" in its teaching. This becomes especially clear when we remember that the apostle Paul, after summing up the main events of Israel's history, wrote, "Now all these things happened to them as examples [types], and they were written for our admonition, upon

7

whom the ends of the ages have come" (1 Cor. 10:11).

Old Testament types may be compared to pictures in a beautifully illustrated book. The New Testament can be compared to the captions in that book that explain the pictures of the Old Testament. If we were to read the captions without ever looking at the pictures to which they refer, we would miss much of the book's inspiration as well as find it much more difficult to understand. In the same way, we Christians lose great blessings and inspiration if we study only the New Testament and try to comprehend its deep truths without referring to the Old Testament, where those very truths are set forth in types and emblems that make them easier to understand.

> The beauty of our God—God the Father, God the Son and God the Holy Spirit—is so transcendent, so wonderful, that no single picture could ever express the depth of truth contained in Him.

8

An *emblem* metaphorically represents an abstract idea or an invisible element and helps to define its general ethical or spiritual meaning.[2] For example, the Holy Spirit is represented by many different symbols or emblems in the Scriptures, which reveal one or more aspects of His Person—of God Himself. There are at least fourteen emblems used in the Scripture to represent various aspects of the Holy Spirit. Each emblem reveals beautiful facets of the Holy Spirit's nature and of His work on earth. Of course, this divine personality can be truly understood only by the revelation of Himself to our hearts. But just as similes and metaphors give our minds a picture to grasp, so emblems help to open our understanding to the revelation of His Person.

Why are there so many types and emblems in the Scriptures? It is because the beauty of our God—God the Father, God the Son and God the Holy Spirit—is so transcendent, so wonderful, that no single picture could ever express the depth of truth contained in Him. The perfection of His character cannot begin to be understood through only one picture, type or emblem. Rather, each symbol gives us a glimpse into one facet of the loveliness of the moral beauty of God. As we discuss a few of these emblems to behold facets of His loveliness, may the power of the Holy Spirit open our eyes to the divine glory they express.

THE DOVE

The Spirit of God descended on Jesus as a dove at His baptism (Matt. 3:16). For those standing on the river bank that day, it must have been a moving experience to see a dove light on Jesus and to hear the voice of God from heaven saying, "This is My beloved Son, in whom I am well pleased" (Matt. 3:17). Although they were not accustomed to witnessing supernatural events, surely they must have thrilled to the presence of God manifested in that hour.

The gentleness of the dove characterizes the personality of the Holy Spirit—the divine character of God. He is never harsh, rude, critical or judgmental. He will convict, correct, instruct, teach and lead, always in the patient gentleness of His divine personality. The dove that Noah sent out of the ark became his servant to bring him news of the earth's condition after the flood. In that same way the Holy Spirit is God serving mankind, bringing us to a knowledge of eternal life and filling us with that life at our request.

The gentleness and servant spirit of the dove show us the character of God that is without a hint of harshness or violence. He gently persuades us of the truth of God's love, then waits for us to invite Him into our lives. He will never coerce us to repent or to obey Him. The Holy Spirit will always deal with mankind in a way that is in character with His gentle nature.

> The abiding presence of the Holy Spirit in the life of the believer is the anointing that gives us the capacity to know the truth and to be set free from every form of deception.

Even in our most painful situations, we dare not think that God allowed our difficulties because of any unkindness in Him. He cannot treat us unkindly, for His divine nature is kind and gentle. Jesus said, "Come to Me, all who are weary and heavy-laden, and I will give you rest. Take My yoke upon you, and learn from Me, for I am gentle and humble in heart; and you shall find rest for your souls" (Matt. 11:28–29, NAS). The Spirit of God, who came to reveal Jesus to us, reflects the gentleness of the dove in all He does in the earth. So the glory of God is revealed according to the

10

nature of the gentle dove used to represent the Holy Spirit.

ANOINTING OIL

God ordained the act of anointing with oil when He instructed Moses to create the anointing oil. The ingredients in the anointing oil are themselves types of the beauty and character of our Lord.[3] The anointing oil symbolizes the Holy Spirit's consecrating grace and guidance for the believer. The Scriptures teach that "the anointing which you received from Him abides in you, and you have no need for anyone to teach you; but as His anointing teaches you about all things, and is true and is not a lie, and just as it has taught you, you abide in Him" (1 John 2:27, NAS).

The abiding presence of the Holy Spirit in the life of the believer is the anointing that gives us the capacity to know the truth and to be set free from every form of deception. It is that facet of God's beautiful character that delivers us from the kingdom of darkness and promises us abundant life in Christ. The Holy Spirit is typified by the anointing oil in order to reveal this precious quality of the glory of God to us.

OIL

Oil is a similar type that gives us understanding of another facet of the Holy Spirit. Oil was used in Bible days as the chief source of illumination apart from the sun. That light symbolizes the power of the Holy Spirit to illuminate truth to us. Jesus taught the parable of the wise virgins who took plenty of oil for their lamps, and the foolish virgins who did not. The foolish virgins were away buying more oil when the bridegroom came. (See Matthew 25:1–13.) Without the oil of the

11

Spirit being plentiful in our lives, we will not be ready when the Bridegroom comes. We must "buy the truth, and do not sell it" as we allow the Holy Spirit to teach us all things so that we will be prepared for the coming of the Lord (Prov. 23:23).

Jesus said," I am the light of the world" (John 8:12). The Holy Spirit filled Him, and He walked as light in the darkness of this world. Then He declared to His disciples, "You are the light of the world" (Matt. 5:14). Only as the Holy Spirit fills our lives can we have truth illumined to us. Then we can reflect the glory of God to the darkened minds of men who do not know God.

FIRE

Many times the Scriptures refer to fire to typify the visible presence of God, according to the second part of our definition of the glory of God. When the children of Israel were in the wilderness, the presence of the Lord was with them in a cloud by day and a pillar of fire by night (Exod. 13:21). Later in history, God declared through His prophet Malachi that the coming of the Lord was like a refiner's fire (Mal. 3:2). John the Baptist preached:

> He that cometh after me is mightier than I, whose shoes I am not worthy to bear: he shall baptize you with the Holy Ghost, and with fire: whose fan is in his hand, and he will thoroughly purge his floor, and gather his wheat into the garner; but he will burn up the chaff with unquenchable fire.
>
> —MATTHEW 3:11–12, KJV

Why fire? Sometimes we fear fire, having seen the devastation it can cause to a home and anything else it touches when it's out of control. Fire has the power to destroy. But that is not the reason God uses fire to symbolize His presence. The work of the Holy Spirit is *creative*, not *chaotic*. It is *redemptive*, not *destructive*. When under control, fire is an invaluable element that provides warmth and light and cleanses and purifies whatever it touches. The Scriptures teach that "God is a consuming fire" (Deut. 4:24). His holiness is the essence of that fire. The fire of God that appeared in the cutting of the covenant with Abraham showed God's approval of Abraham's worship (Gen. 15:17). When Elijah called fire down out of heaven on Mount Carmel, it consumed the sacrifice and proved to the Baal worshipers that the Lord was the true God (1 Kings 18:17–40).

> The Holy Spirit comes as fire to cleanse our temples and to make us holy as He is holy, so that we can reflect His glory in our lives.

When we lift our hearts in worship, we should realize we are standing in the presence of a holy God whose fire can consume the sin in our lives. However, there should be no fear of destruction from that divine fire—only an awesome fellowship in the glory of a holy God.

As our lives are cleansed by fire, so our works will be tried with fire. Everything that is not of eternal value will be burned. We will not need a bonfire to try our works and

13

consume all that is wood, hay and stubble. We will give account of the deeds done, and the very presence of God, the Consuming Fire, will consume all that are works of flesh and our fleshly programs. The apostle Paul declared, "Each man's work will become evident; for the day will show it, because it is to be revealed with fire; and the fire itself will test the quality of each man's work" (1 Cor. 3:13, NAS). Our motivation, our faithfulness and our attitudes will be exposed to the glory of God in the fire of His holiness.

The New Testament declares that "our God is a consuming fire" (Heb. 12:29). The fire of God is a place of safety and security for the believer; it saves us from deception and uncleanness. In that fire we can enjoy the light that casts out the darkness. Walking in that fire results in forgiveness, health and stability. As temples of the Holy Ghost, believers need the cleansing power of the continual fire of God in order to be forgiven and made whole. The Holy Spirit comes as fire to cleanse our temples and to make us holy as He is holy, so that we can reflect His glory in our lives.

14

RAIN

The Scriptures refer to the outpouring of the Holy Spirit as the early and latter rains. "Then shall we know, if we follow on to know the LORD: his going forth is prepared as the morning; and he shall come unto us as the rain, as the latter and former rain unto the earth" (Hos. 6:3, KJV). To a farmer, the latter rains are as equally important as the early rains for the maturing of the harvest. As a faithful husbandman, God watches over His harvest. "See how the farmer [husbandman] waits for the precious fruit of the earth, waiting patiently for it until it receives the early and latter rain" (James 5:7).

God is not building His church in a day. He is patiently working by His Spirit until we grow into maturity to become a glorious church without spot or wrinkle. The life-giving rain that typifies the moving of the Holy Spirit is vital to that growth. The glory of God is most perfectly revealed in mature saints.

Rain speaks of the abundance of the Spirit's supply. The latter rain will bring an abundance of God's presence. "He shall come down like rain upon the grass before mowing, like showers that water the earth. In His days the righteous shall flourish, and abundance of peace, until the moon is no more" (Ps. 72:6–7). We live in anticipation of the coming of the Holy Spirit to our hearts and to His church as life-giving rain.

Understanding the characteristics that we have discussed of the emblems of the Holy Spirit should create in us an awe of the beauty of His Person. To think that it is God's design to infuse us with that beauty—that glory—so that we reflect the divine nature of God's character is almost more than we can comprehend. Yet His desire goes beyond even our holiness. God desires to have intimate communion with us as His children, His family.

Before we continue to search the Scriptures for other significant types and shadows that reveal the glory of God to us, let's look at the Scriptures that give us a glimpse of where all this wonder began. It began before time—in the Godhead.

Chapter 2

Glory in the Godhead

Declaring God's Heart to Mankind

The promise of Scripture to all believers that declares "Christ in you, the hope of glory" was not an afterthought, a makeshift remedy the Godhead had to invent to counteract the destructive plan of Satan when he tempted mankind to disobey God. That promise was fulfilled in the Godhead before time began and is manifest in us as we surrender to the eternal plan of God for our lives. He intended for us to be bearers of His glory from the beginning—from before the foundations of the earth were laid.

What was God's heart for mankind? The great heart of God had a dream that was born out of His need. Although some streams of theology teach that God has no need because of the fact of His self-existence, I believe, by definition, we can establish that God had a need. God is love. Love needs someone who can become a recipient, one who can respond to that love. In order to meet that need, God had a dream for a family that would be made in His image, and into whom He could pour Himself. An important connotation of the word *dream* is "to have aspirations, hopes, ideals and longings for the future." A *dream* is thus a visionary hope that creates deep longing for its fulfillment. That intense desire becomes a motivating force for action. God's dream filled His heart with longing and motivated Him to realize its fulfillment.

> God wanted a family who would *choose* to love Him.

Where did God's wonderful plan to have a family begin, and how does it relate to us today? To answer those questions, let's allow our imaginations to take us back into the eons of eternity, back to the "beginning." We must listen to the triune Godhead as They expressed a deep desire among Themselves. The Scriptures declare that God is love (1 John 4:8). Divine love is not merely an attribute of God's character, but the essence of His Being.

As we have stated, the intrinsic nature of love requires a recipient, one who will respond by choice to the love received. Because of God's longing for someone to respond to His love, They said among Themselves, "Let Us make man in Our image" (Gen. 1:26). God expressed His need by expressing His desire for a family, one into whom He could pour His very nature. His purpose in creating mankind was to have someone with whom to fellowship and share His love. He desired a family who would have His "family spirit" and would choose to respond to His love. He did not create a robot to love Him automatically, for by definition, love does not force someone to respond with love. God wanted a family who would *choose* to love Him.

Having determined to have a family, the triune Godhead took a sworn covenant among Themselves that that dream would be fulfilled. They knew that there would be a terrible cost involved to redeem mankind from the curse his disobedience would bring upon him. The Godhead judicially set full redemption to our account before mankind was ever created or time established. How incalculable must have been the suffering endured when Jesus became the Lamb, slain in the heart of God from the foundation of the world (Rev. 13:8)! The Godhead had to suffer that hurt-love in order for His dream to become a reality. That sacrificial love initiated the fulfillment of God's eternal plan to bring many sons into glory.

In eternity, the three members of the Godhead became totally involved in Their inter-theistic covenant, and swore among Themselves that God's dream would be fulfilled. God later revealed this covenant to Abraham, as the Book of Hebrews tells us: "When God made a promise to Abraham, because He could swear by no one greater, He swore by Himself" (Heb. 6:13). God needed no man to swear by— They swore by each other. Having confirmed the covenant with an oath in eternity, the triune Godhead had initiated among Themselves Their dream for a family.

There was equality among the three members of the Godhead in eternity, as we understand when we read of Christ Jesus: "Who...did not consider it robbery to be equal with God" (Phil. 2:6). Again we read, "In the beginning was the Word, and the Word was with God, and the Word was

19

God" (John 1:1). However, God's plan for a family would affect that equality, as the Father looked beyond Adam's disobedience to make provision for the redemption of mankind, whom They were going to create in Their image.

> Jesus came, not to save us from hell, but to give the Father a family that would reflect the nature of the Father's love.

God's eternal plan was decreed, willed, purposed and predestined before man was created. In the corridors of eternity, Jesus came out of the Godhead as the only begotten Son of God, suffering His *kenosis* to become the "Lamb slain from the foundation of the world" (Rev. 13:8).

That emptying of Himself, of which we read in the second chapter of the Book of Philippians, happened first in eternity before it was manifested on earth in Jesus. It was John, the beloved disciple, as we shall discuss later, who declared, "And the Word became flesh and dwelt among us, and we beheld His glory, the glory as of the only begotten of the Father, full of grace and truth" (John 1:14).

It cost the Godhead inestimable suffering to bring Their love to us. One of our favorite Bible verses reveals the pain involved in bringing God's love to man. As children we learned to quote, "For God so loved the world, that he gave his only begotten Son, that whosoever believeth in him should not perish, but have everlasting life" (John 3:16, KJV). This is a statement of the hurt-love of God. We cannot comprehend

GLORY IN THE GODHEAD

the suffering of God in eternity. God knew that man would fail the love test—that Jesus would have to become the sacrificial Lamb to redeem us unto Himself. Even so, God suffered that incalculable loss. Yet so great was God's need for someone into whom He could pour His love that He proceeded to fulfill His dream to have a family—children who would reflect the glory of the Lamb.

God's hurt-love produced the nature of the Lamb. His family would share His nature—the Lamb spirit of hurt-love. Jesus came, not to save us from hell, but to give the Father a family that would reflect the nature of the Father's love. To accomplish that purpose, Jesus became the Lamb of God, slain in the heart of God. In the types of the Old Testament, we see the suffering heavenly Father each time a man had to choose his own spotless lamb, tie it with a cord and take it to the temple to offer it as a sacrifice.

God the Father is walking with that prepared Pascal Lamb, tied with a cord. He comes with a hurt-love, bringing His Lamb to slaughter in order to redeem us. God's heart is beating with a longing to impart to us the same quality of love the Godhead enjoyed in eternity. Is it any wonder that the highest order of worship found in the Book of Revelation is expressed in the cry, "Worthy is the Lamb who was slain to receive power and riches and wisdom, and strength and honor and glory and blessing!" (Rev. 5:12)?

God gave us a beautiful eightfold picture of His Lamb in the Scriptures in order to portray vividly His plan of redemption of mankind:

1. Peter showed us the lamb of *predestination*. The

apostle Peter wrote, "Redeemed...with the precious blood of Christ, as of a lamb without blemish and without spot. He indeed was foreordained before the foundation of the world" (1 Pet. 1:18–20).

2. We see the lamb of *paradise* in the Garden of Eden, where blood was shed to clothe Adam and Eve with animal skins. Since that time, all sacrificial offerings looked back to the one made by Jehovah-Jesus in the Garden of Eden as well as forward to the sacrifice Christ was to make on Calvary.

3. Abraham and his son Isaac discovered the lamb of *promise* after they ascended the slopes of Mount Moriah to worship. Isaac asked his father, "Where is the lamb for a burnt offering?" Abraham answered, "God will provide for Himself the lamb for a burnt offering" (Gen. 22:7–8).

4. The *Passover* lamb was revealed to the children of Israel the night the death angel visited the firstborn of Egypt (Exodus 12).

5. John the Baptist alluded to the lamb of *pardon* when he saw Jesus coming to the Jordan. He declared, "Behold! The Lamb of God who takes away the sin of the world!" (John 1:29). This was the lamb the Hebrews offered as a sacrifice every morning and evening in their ritual of worship.

6. The lamb of *propitiation* was revealed in the Hebrews' celebration of the Day of Atonement.

7. The lamb of *prophecy* was seen by Isaiah when, under the prophetic inspiration of the Holy Spirit, he declared, "He was led as a lamb to the slaughter" (Isa. 53:7).

8. On the historical cross of Calvary, we saw the lamb *provided.* In the Lord Jesus, God fulfilled every promise, every prophecy, every sacrificial type found in the Bible. That day at Calvary, the Father was still leading His Lamb, all the way to the cross, to bring His dream to pass.

The most wonderful love story ever told is the story of God's love. All mankind is part of God's dream for a family, "Just as He chose us in Him before the foundation of the world...having predestined us to adoption as sons by Jesus Christ to Himself, according to the good pleasure of His will" (Eph. 1:4–5). Every person who would ever be born was in God's mind in eternity when He initiated that dream. Our names were not written in the Lamb's Book of Life when we received Jesus as our Savior—they were written there before the foundation of the world. From eternity God willed that no person on earth should perish. He recorded every name.

God said to Jeremiah the prophet, "Before I formed you in the womb I knew you" (Jer. 1:5). The psalmist David declared:

My frame was not hidden from you
   when I was made in the secret place.
When I was woven together in the depths of the
      earth,
   your eyes saw my unformed body.
All the days ordained for me
   were written in your book
   before one of them came to be.
               —PSALM 139:15–16, NIV

God knew us before we were born, and He ordained that we would have life.

Our names will only be blotted out of the Lamb's Book of Life if we do not *choose* to have the life of God. In the Book of Revelation we read, "He who overcomes shall be clothed in white garments, and I will not blot out his name from the Book of Life" (Rev. 3:5). If we choose to be part of God's family, our names will remain in the Book of Life. If we do not, they will be blotted out. He chose us in Him before the foundation of the world. It is up to us to choose Him now in order to enjoy the eternal life He has provided and be placed into His glory.

Having purposed to fulfill His dream for a family in spite of the cost, God began to unfold His eternal plan by cutting an eon in half and calling it time. He began His work of creation and set mankind in the Garden of Eden. There He fellowshiped with the first ones He created to become the family that would satisfy His heart of love and fulfill His dream. He clothed their nakedness with the light of His glory, so that they had no need of material covering for their bodies. They were perfect in their innocence and enjoyed the purity of unhindered relationship with God and with each other.

But Adam and his wife failed the love test through their disobedience. The voice came walking, seeking him: "Adam, where are you?" We can only imagine the grief that must have filled that voice of love as He sought for Adam that day. The Father's dream, known only to the Godhead, was not revealed to His first man. God couldn't tell Adam of the covenant of the Godhead because of Adam's disobedience that destroyed their relationship—and aborted the relationship with God of all mankind after him.

Centuries later, Moses received the law of God, but that law could not tell us what God's dream was. That which was in God's heart—His dream—was not revealed. The biblical historians, psalmists and poets did not perceive it. Even the prophets were not aware of God's dream. Four hundred dark years after the prophets were silent, what God had planned was not yet revealed.

So God cut out His love in the form of a Person and sent Him to earth as the express image of God. Everything Jesus did, each word He spoke, was to show us the Father's heart. Jesus healed the sick and set the captives free to reveal to us the Father's love. However, just before Jesus left this earth, one of His disciples asked Him to show them the Father— then they would be satisfied. We can almost hear the disappointment in Jesus' answer to His disciples: "Have I been with you so long, and yet you have not known Me, Philip? He who has seen Me has seen the Father" (John 14:9).

Even Jesus could not tell His disciples what was in the

25

Father's heart. They had centered their thoughts on a present earthly kingdom. Jesus said to them, "I still have many things to say to you, but you cannot bear them now" (John 16:12).

He told them He was returning to the Father so that the Counselor could come. The Holy Spirit was part of the plan—He was not an afterthought. He would move inside them and enlighten their minds. "When He, the Spirit of truth, has come, He will guide you into all truth...He will take of what is Mine and declare it to you" (John 16:13–14).

> Everything Jesus did, each word He spoke, was to show us the Father's heart.

Jesus completed the plan for the redemption of mankind through His sacrifice on Calvary. The Holy Spirit was then entrusted to do His precious work in the earth to draw men to God. His task was to put into us what Jesus brought—that divine heartbeat. The throb of God's heart was still to have a family in His image, with His family Spirit—the Spirit of the Lamb—to live and rule with Him. However, no one had yet been able to declare that dream fully to us.

On the Day of Pentecost when the Holy Spirit came, Peter put his telescope to the entire church age, but he didn't see the whole dream of God. He saw bits of its beginning and ending as he prophesied (Acts 2), but he didn't say a word about what was in the Father's heart. He preached to thousands of people in Jerusalem what had been prophesied by Joel: "It shall come to pass in the last days, says God, that I will pour out of My Spirit on all flesh; your sons and your daughters shall prophesy, your young men shall see visions, your old men shall *dream dreams* . . ." (Acts 2:17, emphasis added).

In the original language the phrase *old men* does not refer to age or gender, but rather to *mature saints.* The understanding is that when God begins to pour out His Spirit, mature saints will know the dream of God's heart. And the young men and women will grasp portions of the vision and run to fulfill it as they see the eternal plan that was predestined by the council of God—the Godhead—before the foundation of the world.

The Scriptures give glimpses of this wonderful plan for the redemption of mankind from earliest history. However, that covenant dream was not completely unveiled until God revealed the mystery of the church to the apostle Paul, who declared: "The mystery, which from the beginning of the ages has been hidden in God . . ." (Eph. 3:9). God's dream—His desire for a family—is destined to be fulfilled. God will have a family in His own image, which Jesus Christ, the express image of His Person, revealed to us.

God supernaturally encountered and apprehended for this special purpose the most unlikely man. He had a slaughtering spirit, seemingly farther from the heart of God than anyone could be. Saul of Tarsus was converted and became Paul the Apostle. He was a "full gospel" preacher for a while, until God told him to go to the desert of Arabia. Without conferring with flesh and blood, he obeyed the Spirit's command. During the three years Paul spent in that desert, the Father unfolded to him the great *mystery* that had been hidden since before the foundation of the world.

The apostle Paul later explained to the church at Ephesus what God's eternal plan was:

> To make plain to everyone the administration of this mystery, which for ages past was kept hidden in God...His intent was that now, through the church, the manifold wisdom of God should be made known to the rulers and authorities in the heavenly realms, according to his eternal purpose which he accomplished in Christ Jesus our Lord.
> —EPHESIANS 3:9–11, NIV

Ultimately, God was going to realize His dream for a family through the church, the body of Christ on the earth.

Throughout Paul's christological epistles he reveals the purpose of God for the church. He is going to fill the church with His glory as He works in believers to reveal Christ in them, the hope of glory. God will have a glorious church that will bear His image, with each Christian fulfilling his part of forming the family that God desires. The apostle Paul declared:

> Speaking the truth in love, we will in all things grow up into him who is the Head, that is, Christ. From him the whole body, joined and held together by every supporting ligament, grows and builds itself up in love, as each part does its work.
> —EPHESIANS 4:15–16, NIV

It seems almost too good to be true that God will have a family as described by Paul, especially when we are living in homes and churches that seem to be full of "spots and wrinkles." Why is there such a disparity between what God intends for His family and who we are now? Where is the

28

unity, the love, the Christlike humility that characterize the glory of God revealed in Jesus Christ?

The answers to these questions will help us close the gap between God's dream—that of a family that will reflect His glory—and the reality of the people we are today. We must believe that God's dream will be fulfilled as He purposed it from eternity. He has promised, "I will put my laws in their minds and write them on their hearts. I will be their God, and they will be my people. No longer will a man teach his neighbor, or a man his brother, saying, 'Know the Lord' because they will all know me, from the least of them to the greatest" (Heb. 8:10–11, NIV).

God's eternal plan will be realized in our individual lives, in our homes and ultimately in the church as we are conformed to the image of Christ through the working of the Holy Spirit in us. This Third Person of the Godhead has dedicated Himself to His divine task of bringing home a bride for the Son of God. He will succeed in His task, presenting a glorious church to Him, without spot or wrinkle.

If we are to be part of God's heart desire for a family that will reflect His glory, we will need to cultivate a relationship with the Holy Spirit, understanding who He is and cooperating with Him as He works to fulfill God's desire for mankind.

Chapter 3

The Glory of God in Creation

The Servant Delivering God's Dream

Many theologians from various denominations concur that the Holy Spirit is the most neglected and least understood Person of the Godhead. Many are reevaluating church doctrine, dogma and practice to attempt to bring their theology—the understanding of God—into balance as the true Trinitarians that they claim to be. Church fathers from earliest times wrote treatises defining and describing the Persons and work of the Father and of Christ Jesus, the Son, but few have emphasized the precious Person and work of the Holy Spirit. Many Christians are not fully aware, for example, of the wonderful work of the Holy Spirit in Creation.

At the turn of the twentieth century, a worldwide movement of the Holy Spirit that birthed the Pentecostals brought to prominence the charismatic gifts of the Holy Spirit—valid gifts to the church today. Later, the Charismatic movement

31

included many people from other denominations who experienced the baptism of the Holy Spirit accompanied by glossalalia. The phenomenal growth of the Charismatic congregations around the world has attracted the attention of many denominational Christians.

Yet many Christians, when asked where the Holy Spirit is first mentioned in the Scriptures, quote references in the New Testament. Some even cite Acts 2 as the first mention of the Holy Spirit. It surprises them when they are asked to turn to Genesis 1 to see the first mention of this Third Person of the Godhead.

While we cannot devote the space in this volume to an in-depth study of the Holy Spirit, we need to understand His divine assignment in revealing the glory of God so that we can cooperate with Him as He works in our lives to make us reflectors of that glory. (I have published my life study of the Holy Spirit in two volumes.)[1]

The precious Holy Spirit, the Third Person of the God-head, is the *pneuma*—the divine breath of God. Scriptures teach that He is the divine agent in Creation. In Genesis 1 we read:

> And the earth was formless and void, and darkness was over the surface of the deep: and the Spirit of God was moving over the surface of the waters.
>
> —GENESIS 1:2, NAS

Though it is impossible for finite man to enter into the divine dynamics of creation, we understand that when God declared, "Let there be...", the Holy Spirit was there, hovering over the earth and fulfilling every Word of God. The psalmist declared many centuries later:

> The heavens are telling of the glory of God;
> And their expanse is declaring the work of His hands.
> Day to day pours forth speech,
> And night to night reveals knowledge.
>
> —PSALM 19:1–2, NAS

The prophet Isaiah had a vision of the seraphim in heaven around the throne of God. They were calling out, "Holy, Holy, Holy, is the LORD of hosts, the whole earth is full of His glory" (Isa. 6:3, NAS).

After the fall of man in the garden, God cursed the ground so that it would bring forth briars and thorns. Man would have to eat bread by the sweat of his face (Gen. 3:18–19). The apostle Paul declares that all of creation is groaning in the hope that it "will be set free from its slavery to corruption into the freedom of the glory of the children of God" (Rom. 8:21, NAS). Yet even in our fallen state, with creation suffering under the curse, we can still behold the glory of God in every star and tree and flower, in the majesty of the mountains and the oceans and all that He created. Scientists are continually discovering new secrets of life as God created it in every species that exists on earth today.

And as far as the crowning jewel of creation is concerned, mankind is still a wonder that is being explored physically, mentally and spiritually in order to unravel the glory of God's creation. Again it was the psalmist who contemplated this wonder when he declared:

> What is man, that Thou dost take thought of him?
> And the son of man, that Thou dost care for him?
> Yet Thou hast made him a little lower than God,
> And dost crown him with glory and majesty!
> —PSALM 8:4–5, NAS

THE NEW CREATION

As the Holy Spirit was the agent in all of creation, so He became the Life-giver in the new creation. Jesus taught Nicodemus that "unless one is born again, he cannot see the kingdom of God" (John 3:3). When Nicodemus asked how it was possible for a man to enter into his mother's womb and be born again, Jesus answered, "Most assuredly, I say to you, unless one is born of water and the Spirit, he cannot enter the kingdom of God" (v. 5).

I had been born again for twenty years before I understood what really happened to me in my conversion experience. I had taught the Word without a real revelation of what salvation involved. After I was healed and baptized in the Holy Spirit, my Teacher began to explain the Book to me. He asked me if I wanted Him to explain the impartation of the living seed.

I was so embarrassed. I said, "Jesus, you mean I don't even know that? I have been preaching for so long, and I don't even know what happened to me when I got saved! I am going back to first base for sure."

34

He comforted me by saying, "Daughter, you don't tell your children about the birds and bees when they are babies. Now *you* are old enough for Me to tell you what happened to you in the new birth."

In a vision, I saw the virgin Mary kneeling before the angel of the Lord. I saw the Holy Spirit overshadowing her, and I understood that in the same way He overshadowed Mary, He had overshadowed my spirit when I was born again. Just as He had impregnated her with Jesus, He had impregnated me by placing the incorruptible seed of God in my spirit. The reality of salvation is that God is living in our spirits from the moment we are born again. That is why we truly become a new creation through the power of the Holy Spirit.

> I believe the Holy Spirit is working now to cleanse the church in order that believers might reflect the glory of God to the lost around the world.

As we have mentioned, it is the divine task of the Third Person of the Godhead to bring home the family of God, changed into the image of God. There have been many outpourings of the Holy Spirit since the Day of Pentecost as the Servant has been faithful in His part of fulfilling God's desire for a glorious church. In every move of God, the Holy Spirit has restored truths to the church and empowered men and women to declare the gospel in a way that has resulted in a great ingathering of souls.

35

I believe that there is coming a great End-Time revival that will eclipse all we have seen in the history of the church. As I wrote in my book *The Next Move of God,* I believe the Holy Spirit is working now to cleanse the church in order that believers might reflect the glory of God to the lost around the world.[2] Then He is going to cause us to reap a great End-Time harvest of souls.

THE HOLY SPIRIT AS
BRIDE-SEEKER IN TYPE

The glory of God revealed in His desire for a family is the ultimate desire of the Father. It was His intention from the beginning, and He will not be disappointed. Not only is the Holy Spirit the breath of God in creation and the life-giver in the new creation, but He is also the servant devoted to bringing a bride home for the Son. A beautiful type of this aspect of the Holy Spirit's work is given to us in the story of Abraham's search for a wife for his son Isaac. (See Genesis 24.)

When Abraham chose to seek a bride for his son Isaac, he called his servant and made him take an oath that he would go and search for a girl to be a bride for Isaac. The servant covenanted with the father to follow certain guidelines in order to secure a suitable bride for Isaac. Although we know this story to contain actual historical events, it has a larger significance as a type and shadow to reveal the desire of our heavenly Father to seek a bride for His only Son in the earth.

THE SPIRIT OF THE SERVANT

It is significant that throughout the entire account of this historical narrative, the servant never refers to himself by name, but simply as the servant of Abraham. His name is never mentioned by the writer of Genesis. Bible commentators have said that his identity was *probably* that of Eliezer of Damascus—a conclusion drawn from earlier references to Abram's servant. Thus the spirit of the servant prevails in accomplishing the divine destiny of bringing a bride for the son.

In this beautiful analogy, the servant represents the Holy Spirit, who has covenanted with the Father to secure a bride who is suitable for His Son. The focus and divine passion of the Holy Spirit is the same—to be a servant to the Father and prepare a bride for the Son. All that He does as the agent of redemption for the born-again experience of every believer—His cleansing, sanctifying and delivering power as well as the giving of supernatural gifts—has the supreme goal of preparing a corporate bride for Jesus Christ.

CHOSEN FROM AMONG HIS OWN PEOPLE

Abraham asked his servant to get a bride for his son Isaac from among his own people. This is an important understanding because I do not believe everyone will be a part of the bride of Christ. Brides *choose* to be brides—it is not an *appointment* but a *relationship* of choice. Men should not have a problem considering becoming a *bride of Christ.* Women are supposed to be *sons of God.* Life in God is free of gender restrictions. The bride relationship is one of intimacy, which results from life choices we make to follow the Servant to receive our Isaac. According to this analogy, it seems that the bride is to be chosen from among the family of the father—or the church.

THE BRIDE-TO-BE COMES TO THE WELL.

The servant prayed and asked God to let the girl who was to be the bride come to the well where he was. Later he asked her to draw water for him *and* to draw water for his camels also. Before he finished speaking, Rebekah came to the well to draw water. In Scripture, a well of water often typifies the Word of God. Allegorically, coming to the well means that we draw living water from the Scriptures, which nourishes divine life within us—and then we provide that divine life to others. This is a requirement for being a part of the bride of Christ. The bride of Christ will be drawing water from the well at evening, at the end of the day.

A JOURNEY WITH TEN CAMELS

The servant took ten camels for the journey to seek a bride. Ten is a number representing the redeemed church. For example, Jesus told the parables of the ten virgins and the ten coins, illustrating the redemption of the church.

With gifts from the father, Abraham's servant left home to begin his mission to return with a bride for the son. In that same way, the Holy Spirit left heaven with gifts from the Father to seek throughout the earth for a bride for the Son of God.

Camels don't ride well. I have tried it. When I was in Egypt I went for a camel ride. Not knowing that you are supposed to ride in the valley of the hump, I sat on the top of the hump. That was miserable. The Egyptian camel owner yelled at me and shoved me down into the valley of the hump. As I settled between the humps, I decided to lean back against the hump— just as you would lean against the back of a chair. I didn't know that was a signal to the camel to kneel so that the rider could get off. The camel lunged forward onto his knees, and I had to fighting to keep from flying over his neck! All the while the Egyptian camel owner was screaming something I couldn't understand. Finally the camel and I came to terms, and we went for a short ride during the time that remained.

Camels represent the trials and tests we must endure on the way home to our Isaac. Too many times people want to rebuke their "camels" or shoot them. But if they do, they will have no way to get home to their Bridegroom. The trial of our faith is precious and redemptive according to the Scriptures (1 Pet. 1:7). Those dusty miles of jogging up and down on a dirty, smelly camel, perhaps for days, were a trial to Rebekah. But she endured it and reached the prize, alighting with joy from her trial when she lifted up her eyes and beheld Isaac at her journey's end.

> Too many times people want to rebuke their "camels" or shoot them. But if they do, they will have no way to get home to their Bridegroom.

39

THE BRIDE MUST CHOOSE.

Rebekah had to make her choice to go with the servant in spite of her family's pleas that she wait awhile. They wanted her to consider her decision for several days before she decided to leave all she knew and loved to follow this man who promised her such a wonderful bridegroom. The servant had presented gifts from the father to her and her family. They were enough to let her realize that this was a wealthy man and an honorable one whose son she desired to know. When her family heard her decision to go with the servant, they blessed her. So she mounted the camel and began her journey under the protective care of the servant, who knew the way home to the bridegroom. So too we can trust the precious Holy Spirit to protect us and lead us along our journey until we have come home to our heavenly Bridegroom.

The Bridegroom is worth the journey.

When she saw Isaac in the shadows and asked the servant who he was, Rebekah was no longer interested in the gifts she had received. The trials of the journey no longer mattered to her. She had eyes only for the beloved bridegroom. It was then that she covered her face with a veil and allowed the servant to present her to the bridegroom. Then he took her into his mother's tent and she became his wife.

It is important to realize that the Holy Spirit has given us wonderful supernatural gifts to enable us and help us in our journey. But the gifts of the Spirit are not intended to give us a big ministry or make us great personally. They are intended to help show us the way to our heavenly Bridegroom. The closer we get to Him, the less interest we will show in the gifts. Our eyes will be fixed on the Bridegroom Himself, arousing our passion to become one with Him—to be His bride.

When the glory of God is revealed to us in that relationship, we will no longer be satisfied with ministry or gifts or anything else we have discovered along our journey. The love of a bride for her bridegroom will be all consuming. In that relationship new life will be conceived.

DISCOVERING THE PURPOSES OF GOD

The purposes of God are realized in the consummation of our love relationship with the Son. Christ in us, the hope of glory, will be revealed to the world to bring forth life in others as we give ourselves totally to Him.

We choose to leave all to follow the Holy Spirit on a trouble-filled journey until we reach the place where the Bridegroom dwells. Only then will our hearts be satisfied, and we will become bearers of His glory.

Pictures such as this beautiful love story that reveals to us how to follow the Holy Spirit are found throughout the Scriptures. They give us principles to embrace if we want to truly have a revelation of the glory of God and be placed, ultimately, in His glory. They reveal the lovely character of God in His moral beauty, and they demonstrate His great heart's desire for relationship with His people.

41

As we follow this thread of truth concerning the glory of God through the Scriptures, your capacity for understanding and being bearers of that glory will be enlarged. Of course, your finite soul can never expect to fully comprehend an infinite God. But as you enter into covenant relationship with Him, His Word promises that you will be changed from glory to glory by beholding His face (2 Cor. 3:18). Our desperate need for change, as we have seen, is a result of the fall of mankind. Because our first parents yielded to the taunts of the tempter in the Garden of Eden, we became slaves to sin.

A closer look at the origin of *iniquity*, as revealed in the Scriptures, will help us understand the source of our difficulty to become true bearers of the glory of God.

Chapter 4

Glory in Heavenly Creatures

Exposing Lucifer, the Morning Star

Whenever the Scriptures open the curtain to the heavens where God dwells on His throne, we are ushered into a divinely ordered worship service beyond description and human understanding. Though they are few in number, both the Old and New Testaments recount experiences of individuals who received a divine revelation of God in His heavenly abode. It is difficult to read these passages without a wonder and reverence filling our hearts with a holy fear of God.

ISAIAH'S
VISION OF HEAVEN

The prophet Isaiah describes one of these holy revelations of the throne of God and the powerful impact it had on his own life:

In the year that King Uzziah died, I saw the Lord sitting on a throne, high and lifted up, and the train of His robe filled the temple. Above it stood seraphim; each one had six wings: with two he covered his face, with two he covered his feet, and with two he flew. And one cried to another and said: "Holy, Holy, Holy is the LORD of hosts; the whole earth is full of His glory!" And the posts of the door were shaken by the voice of him who cried out, and the house was filled with smoke. So I said: "Woe is me, for I am undone! Because I am a man of unclean lips, and I dwell in the midst of a people of unclean lips; for my eyes have seen the King, the LORD of hosts."

—ISAIAH 6:1–5

When Isaiah glimpsed the other-worldly, spiritual domain of the King of kings, he experienced the holiness of pure worship of angelic beings. So stark was the contrast between the holiness of God they proclaimed in their angelic purity and Isaiah's own humanity that even Isaiah, a prophet of God, had to declare, "Woe is me…I am a man of unclean lips." This spokesman for God in the earth had to acknowledge his own impurity when God opened his eyes to behold Him as He really is. Yet that was not the end of the matter. As part of receiving a revelation of this great God who is love, Isaiah was provided with a divine remedy for his uncleanness:

Then one of the seraphim flew to me, having in his hand a live coal which he had taken with the tongs from the altar. And he touched my mouth with it, and said: "Behold, this has touched your lips; your iniquity is taken away, and your sin purged."

—Isaiah 6:6–7

So many astounding aspects of Isaiah's experience could be studied with great interest. Consider an altar of fire that existed in heaven, and angels who could not touch the coals upon it without tongs. Consider the cleansing power of that coal to remove the iniquity of Isaiah by simply touching the lips of that contrite prophet who had acknowledged his uncleanness. Perhaps one of the most awesome considerations is the new divine commission that Isaiah received through this experience:

Also I heard the voice of the Lord, saying: "Whom shall I send, and who will go for Us?" Then I said, "Here am I! Send me."

—Isaiah 6:8

The command Isaiah received was in keeping with his prophetic anointing that he should go and tell the people of God the word of the Lord for them. In this case the word of the Lord was not pleasant because of the disobedience of the people of God. Isaiah received the empowering he needed through his vision of the glory of God to obey the voice of God.

ANGELIC VISITATIONS IN THE WORD

Although there are not many instances recorded in the Scriptures of open visions of heaven, there are quite a few instances when men and women received an angelic visitation.

45

The angel of the Lord appeared to many people as recorded in both Old and New Testament passages. Always the divine visitation evoked awe and worship from the person who received such a heavenly revelation. There were times when the angels had to warn someone not to worship them, but to worship God alone. (See Revelation 19:10.) The glory of God in the presence of a heavenly creature was so awesome that human hearts unwittingly responded in worship to them. Without exception, these angelic beings refused to receive worship that belonged to God alone.

> The exquisite, abandoned response of gratitude that fills a heart with desire to thank and praise His Creator for giving him his being is intrinsic to the redeemed soul.

46

When Daniel waited before God, confessing the sin of God's people, he received a visitation from the angel Gabriel. This angelic visitor came with a divine message from God to give understanding to Daniel regarding his petitions. As we know, these revelations were more far reaching than Daniel's current situation, and they are studied by many today to help us understand what God's plans are for our future. Angelic visitations bring a new revelation of the glory of God and His heart for His people.

There were angelic visitations surrounding the coming of Christ to earth—the angel that appeared to Zacharias, the father of John the Baptist; to Mary, the mother of Jesus; and to Joseph, His earthly father. Angels appeared to shepherds to herald the birth of Christ as well. Wonder and awe gripped those who saw these divine manifestations of the glory of God and received words of comfort and instruction from angelic beings.

John the Revelator gave us a moving description of heaven and the worship that occurs around the throne of God. He describes what he saw through a door standing open in heaven:

> Immediately I was in the Spirit; and behold, a throne set in heaven, and One sat on the throne. And He who sat there was like a jasper and a sardius stone in appearance; and there was a rainbow around the throne, in appearance like an emerald...Whenever the living creatures give glory and honor and thanks to Him who sits on the throne, who lives forever and ever, the twenty-four elders fall down before Him who sits on the throne and worship Him who lives forever and ever, and cast their crowns before the throne, saying, "You are worthy, O Lord, to receive glory and honor and power: for You created all things, and by Your will they exist and were created."
>
> —REVELATION 4:2–3, 9–11

It is important to notice the motive of these worshiping elders. They declare the worthiness of God to receive all their worship because He is responsible for the existence of all things. It is by His will that all things exist—including them. This is an important concept to understand, especially in the face of skeptics who question the character of a God who desires worship from His creation. Their contention is that God must be egotistical to desire worship. This wicked conclusion is drawn, as we shall see, from the misconception of our relationship with God, the Creator of all things.

> If you believe you have a *bigger devil* than you have an *all-powerful God,* you will believe the devil's lies that you cannot be a victorious Christian or gain victory over the devil.

The exquisite, abandoned response of gratitude that fills a heart with desire to thank and praise His Creator for giving him his being is intrinsic to the redeemed soul. One has only to read the Psalms to gain this perspective. The psalmist cries out, "Bless the LORD, O my soul; and all that is within me, bless His holy name" (Ps. 103:1). In another verse, the psalmist exclaims, "Let everything that has breath praise the LORD" (Ps. 150:6). The exuberant cry of a healthy soul acknowledges that all he is and has was given to him by His Creator.

It was Satan in the Garden of Eden that first cast dispersions on God's character, accusing Him of not wanting mankind to become as gods themselves. As we look closer at this tempter, we will learn how great a place true worship must have in our lives if we are to know God, reflect His glory in our lives and be a part of His eternal purposes forever.

48

LUCIFER'S ORIGIN

The name *Lucifer* comes from the Hebrew word *helel*, which means "morning star or light-bringer, one who spreads brightness." This title rightly belongs to Christ, according to His own words:

> I, Jesus, have sent My angel to testify to you these things in the churches. I am the Root and the Offspring of David, *the Bright and Morning Star.*
> —REVELATION 22:16, EMPHASIS ADDED

Satan is only referred to as *Lucifer* in one passage in Isaiah:

> How you are fallen from heaven, O Lucifer, son of the morning! How you are cut down to the ground, you who weakened the nations!
> —ISAIAH 14:12

49

In all other instances he is called *Satan* or *the devil* most often, though he has other titles as well.

We are all familiar with various caricatures of the devil that are common, even among Christians. This arch-rival of God is pictured as a red monster with a tail and a pitchfork in many forms of art. Yet, in reality, he still appears as an angel of light with the intention to deceive people to follow him (2 Cor. 11:14). Among those who believe in the existence of a devil, some discount his power and activity, while others make him as powerful for evil as God is for good. Neither picture of Satan is accurate, and both misconceptions can negatively affect our lives.

If you do not regard him as the real threat that he is to your life in God, you will be "ignorant of his wiles." The Scriptures warn us not to be ignorant of the devil's intentions and strategies if we are to be victorious Christians. On the other hand, if you believe you have a *bigger devil* than you have an *all-powerful God,* you will believe the devil's lies that you cannot be a victorious Christian or gain victory over the devil.

For these reasons, and because the glory of God was once reflected powerfully in the angelic creation known as Lucifer, we need to understand what the Scriptures teach about this fallen creature. Satan desires to receive worship for himself (Matt. 4:8–10). He has intense hatred for humanity and is determined to destroy all mankind (John 10:10; 1 Pet. 5:8). These wicked characteristics compel us to understand who he really is in order to be victorious over his evil plans. His wicked character gives us vital insight by contrast into the character and nature of the glory of God.

50

Two Old Testament passages that describe Lucifer, according to most Bible scholars, are found in prophetic passages dealing both with current events and the larger realm of prophetic inspiration that applies to spiritual realities that govern those events.

For example, Merrill F. Unger explains that in the passage of Isaiah 14, Lucifer or Satan is seen as "a symbolical representation of the king of Babylon in his pride, splendor and fall."[1]

Unger continues his explanation by saying:

> The passage goes beyond the Babylonian prince
> and invests Satan, who, at the head of this present
> world system, is the real though invisible power

behind the successive world rulers of Tyre, Babylon, Persia, Greece and Rome.

This far-reaching passage goes beyond human history and marks the beginning of sin in the universe and the fall of Satan and the pristine, sinless spheres before the creation of man. Similarly Ezekiel (Ezek. 28:12–14), under the figure of the king of Tyre, likewise traces the fall of Satan and the corruption of his power and glory. In the Ezekiel passage Satan's glorious and splendid unfallen state is described. In Isaiah 14 his fall is depicted. In both passages representation is not of Satan as confined to his own person but working in and consummating his plans through earthly kings and rulers who take to themselves divine honors and who, whether they actually know this or not, rule in the spirit and under the aims of Satan.[2]

51

With this understanding, let's look at the biblical description of Lucifer as a beautiful created being in heaven:

> You were the seal of perfection, full of wisdom and perfect in beauty. You were in Eden, the garden of God; Every precious stone was your covering: The sardius, topaz, and diamond, beryl, onyx, and jasper, sapphire, turquoise, and emerald with gold. The workmanship of your timbrels and pipes was prepared for you on the day you were created. You were the anointed cherub who covers.
>
> —EZEKIEL 28:12–14

While we may have difficulty relating perhaps to a heavenly creature in whom every precious stone was his covering, we can imagine the brilliance of colored light that must have emanated from him. It has been suggested that the precious stones—sardius, topaz, diamond, beryl, onyx, jasper, sapphire, turquoise, and emerald—reflected the light of God's glory around the throne. We love to look at light reflected and refracted in semi-precious and precious stones that have been set into gold and formed into necklaces, bracelets and jewelry of all kinds. Perhaps this will help us imagine the beauty of a creature that was covered entirely with every kind of precious stone. How did the perfect light of God shine from this one whose name means "morning star" or "spreading brightness"?

Lucifer is further described as walking in the midst of the stones of fire. Perhaps this is descriptive of the fiery light of God reflecting from the precious stones and all around. We still value a precious stone according to the "fire" that it contains. The depth of light we can see in a diamond increases its value. And God is called a consuming fire (Deut. 4:24). His very nature shines forth with all the properties of fire.

Isaiah describes the "workmanship of your timbrels and pipes" as well, which seemed to emanate from this heavenly creature. Heavenly sounds and sights that defy description by human minds seem to apply to this anointed cherub. I like to imagine all the orchestral sounds we know—the woodwinds, the brass, the violins, cellos and percussion—along with musical sounds we have never heard, sounding forth their beautiful music in the presence of the throne of

God through this angelic being. With the heavenly sounds was the dazzling light reflecting from every precious stone, all declaring God's glory to all creatures and providing a covering of pure worship that was truly heavenly.

Because Lucifer is referred to as the cherub that covers around the throne of God, and because music was an integral part of his being, he is considered to have been a leader of worship in the presence of God. It is certainly true from Scripture that no created being who stayed in the presence of God could be characterized apart from worship. Both angelic and human creations as seen in heaven are engaged in praise and worship of a holy God. But something happened in Lucifer—described by the prophets:

> The church will be a beautiful and accurate manifestation of the glory of God in the earth as lively stones that are built into a unified building to reveal the presence of God to the world.

53

You were perfect in your ways from the day you were created, till iniquity was found in you. By the abundance of your trading you became filled with violence within, and you sinned...Your heart was lifted up because of your beauty; you corrupted your wisdom for the sake of your splendor; I cast you to the ground . . .

—EZEKIEL 28:15–17

Isaiah pictures the devastating demise of this glorious creature:

> How you have fallen from heaven, O Lucifer, son of the morning! How you are cut down to the ground, you who weakened the nations! For you have said in your heart, "I will ascend into heaven, I will exalt my throne above the stars of God . . . I will be like the Most High." Yet you shall be brought down to Sheol, to the lowest depths of the Pit.
>
> —ISAIAH 14:12–15

While the Scriptures do not clarify how or why iniquity was found in Lucifer, they do clearly describe the essence of the iniquity—he desired to become like the Most High, to ascend and place his throne above the stars of God. Ezekiel says that Lucifer's heart was lifted up because of his beauty. It is easy to deduce that he desired to receive worship that belonged only to God, and that the pride of his heart was his downfall.

The next time we encounter Satan, he is in the Garden of Eden, tempting and deceiving the crowning glory of God's creation—mankind. And what was his strategy? To entice them to become as gods themselves by eating the fruit that God had forbidden. He dared to defame God's character and blaspheme His Word: "Has God indeed said? . . . You will not surely die . . . You will be like God" (Gen. 3:1, 4–5). He was still trying to rob God of His glory.

He succeeded in robbing mankind of the glory of God that covered Adam and Eve so that they did not perceive their own nakedness.

That Lucifer is still craving to be worshiped is clear throughout the Old Testament as he inspired the nations, and even God's people, to worship idols instead of the living God. Bible scholars trace the history of idolatry throughout Scripture and comment on the idolatrous bent that is common to mankind:

> There is ever in the human mind a craving for visible forms to express religious conceptions, and this tendency does not disappear with the acceptance, or even with the constant recognition, of pure spiritual truths. Idolatry originally meant the worship of idols, or the worship of false gods by means of idols, but came to mean among the Old Testament Hebrews any worship of false gods, whether by images or otherwise, and finally the worship of Yahweh through visible symbols. (See Hosea 8:5–6; 10:5.) And ultimately in the New Testament idolatry came to mean, not only the giving to any creature or human creation the honor or devotion which belonged to God alone, but the giving to any human desire a precedence over God's will (1 Cor. 10:14; Gal. 5:20; Col. 3:5; 1 Pet. 4:3).[3]

55

In Jesus' temptation in the wilderness, Satan plainly asked Jesus to fall down and worship him in exchange for "all the kingdoms of the world and their glory" (Matt. 4:8–9). Satan has not changed in his ambition to receive the worship that belongs only to God. He is still inspiring music that is dedicated to him, providing modern-day idols for people to worship and attempting to destroy people's lives through the power of sin as he did in the Garden of Eden. Jesus' response to Satan's challenge was clear: "It is written, 'You shall worship the LORD your God, and Him only you shall serve'" (Matt. 4:10).

WORSHIP RESTORED

Through the church, the worship that Satan stole from God in his terrible betrayal that resulted in his being cast out of heaven and doomed to eternal destruction is being restored. It is the apostle Peter who pictures the church "as living stones," who "are being built up a spiritual house, a holy priesthood, to offer up spiritual sacrifices acceptable to God through Jesus Christ" (1 Pet. 2:5).

The prophet Isaiah used this language of precious stones to comfort God's people:

> O you afflicted one, tossed with tempest, and not comforted, behold, I will lay your stones with colorful gems, and lay your foundations with sapphires. I will make your pinnacles of rubies, your gates of crystal, and all your walls of precious stones...In righteousness you shall be established; you shall be far from oppression... for it shall not come near you.
>
> —ISAIAH 54:11–12, 14

Righteousness is linked in Scripture to the beauty of precious stones. They show forth the character and nature of God in all His glory. So the church will be a beautiful and accurate manifestation of the glory of God in the earth as lively stones that are built into a unified building to reveal the presence of God to the world. We will reflect His holiness and demonstrate the fire of His love in the same way that all of heaven worships Him, who alone is worthy of all praise and honor and power. As true worship is restored to the church through deep humility of heart, the glory of the Lord will shine through His people in such a powerful way that the lost will be saved. In my book *Worship Him,* I wrote:

> The apostle Peter declared to the church, "But ye are a chosen generation, a royal priesthood, an holy nation, a peculiar people; that ye should shew forth the praises of him who hath called you out of darkness into his marvelous light" (1 Pet. 2:9). The light of God will shine through His people as we demonstrate the praises of God in the earth. This is a corporate responsibility of a people "which in time past were not a people, but are now the people of God" (v. 10)...We have defined worship in spirit and in truth simply as the expression of a heart yielded to the Holy Spirit and worshiping according to the truth of the Word. It involves believers honoring and adoring God as the Holy Spirit inspires them according to the pattern He has revealed to us in the Scriptures.

Just as in the beginning of time, when the Spirit and the Word brought order out of chaos, both the Spirit and the Word must be present in our worship expressions for divine order to be established. The Spirit brooded over the face of the earth, and the Word spoke order into creation. (See Genesis 1:1–5.) So divine worship is dependent upon the Spirit and the Word operating in the midst of the worshiping congregation.[4]

As individuals are redeemed and restored to their relationship with God, forming the body of Christ in the earth, so worship will be restored. It will be the deepest expression of that relationship, and will bring fulfillment to our hearts as well as to the heart of God. To the degree that we experience true worship, we will be set free from the deceptions of the Lucifer who vies for our worship, tempting us with idolatrous substitutes for the true worship of God alone.

Satan's fate is certain—he was defeated at Calvary and will one day be cast into the lake of fire and brimstone to be tormented day and night forever (Rev. 20:10). I believe that one day there will be no more trace that there has ever been a devil. All of his destruction in the earth and in our lives will be redeemed by the love of the Son of God, and we will enjoy the bliss of eternity as God intended it from the beginning. All of creation will rejoice in that day and show forth the glory of our God as well.

Ever since Satan's attempt to rob mankind of the glory of God, God has been seeking to reveal Himself to man and find ways of showing forth His glory to His beloved creation. As we trace the working of His longing heart through the Scriptures, we will understand more clearly the loving heart of God and learn to reverence His glory.

The costly redemption of mankind has been in process ever since the fall of man in the Garden of Eden. God chose men who became patriarchs of faith to whom He could reveal His glory and restore a part of what mankind had lost in the tragedy of the fall. Faithfully He led them to a place of understanding of His great heart, which longed for the covenant relationship of Father and children to be restored.

As individuals are redeemed and restored to their relationship with God, forming the body of Christ in the earth, so worship will be restored.

59

Chapter 5

The Glory
Revealed to Patriarchs

A Covenant-Keeping God

When God promised Abraham that his seed would out-number the stars, the Scriptures declare that Abraham "believed in the LORD, and He accounted it to him for righteousness" (Gen. 15:6). Then when God promised to give Abraham the land of Canaan, Abraham asked God how he would know that he would possess it.

ABRAHAM CUTS
COVENANT WITH GOD

It was then that God commanded Abraham to prepare a sac-rifice, a type of blood covenant that God Himself would enter into with this man whom he had called to be the father of His nation:

So He said to him, "Bring Me a three-year-old

heifer, a three-year-old female goat, a three-year-old ram, a turtledove, and a young pigeon." Then he brought all these to Him and cut them in two, down the middle, and placed each piece opposite the other; but he did not cut the birds in two...Now when the sun was going down, a deep sleep fell upon Abram; and behold, horror and great darkness fell upon him...And it came to pass, when the sun went down and it was dark, that behold, there appeared a smoking oven and a burning torch that passed between those pieces. On the same day the LORD made a covenant with Abram, saying: "To your descendants I have given this land, from the river of Egypt to the great river, the River Euphrates..."

—GENESIS 15: 9–10, 12, 17–18

62

Can we even imagine the wonder of God speaking to man in the way He did to Abram? When the glory of the presence of God came to cut a covenant with this man, he had to be put into a deep sleep. God walked among the pieces of the sacrifice Abram had prepared as a smoking oven and burning torch. He made His promise to Abram—one He could not break. His people would inherit a Promised Land, though it would be many generations after Abram had died.

The sacredness of this blood covenant, of course, lies in the fact that it is a type and shadow of the covenant Christ would establish through the shedding of His blood on Calvary for the remission of our sins. All who would accept this sacrifice could become sons of God and inherit all that relationship promises as revealed in the Scriptures.

You might consider the type inaccurate, since Christ was not torn in two as the animals were in the sacrifice prepared by Abram on that night. Even the prophets who prophesied Christ's death declared that not one of His bones would be broken.

But have you ever thought of Jesus' words from the cross, "My God, my God, why hast thou forsaken me?" Jesus was severed from the oneness He had enjoyed with the Father from the beginning. That divine relationship between God and God, between God and the Son of Man, was broken at Calvary. It was an incomprehensible tearing and rending of the heart of God as He descended into hell to become our sin offering. The Third Person of the Godhead, the Holy Spirit, went to get Christ, to bring Him back and raise Him up. He is the same Holy Spirit who quickens us when we are dead in trespasses and sin and makes us alive (Eph. 2:1).

63

Circumcision was to be the seal of the blood covenant God made with Abraham and all his descendants. (See Genesis 17.) Every male child was to be circumcised as a sign of the covenant God was making with Abraham to give them the land of promise. The New Testament teaches that we must experience a circumcision of the heart, a cutting away of fleshly desires and carnal ways of thinking. The apostle Paul declared:

> For he is not a Jew who is one outwardly, nor is circumcision that which is outward in the flesh; but he is a Jew who is one inwardly; and circumcision is that of the heart, in the Spirit, not in the

letter; whose praise is not from men but from God.

—ROMANS 2:28–29

This same apostle instructed the church at Colossae:

For in Him [Christ] dwells all the fullness of the Godhead bodily; and you are complete in Him, who is the head of all principality and power. In Him you were also circumcised with the circumcision made without hands, by putting off the body of the sins of the flesh, by the circumcision of Christ.

—COLOSSIANS 2:9–11

And to the Galatians he explained:

For in Christ Jesus neither circumcision nor uncircumcision avails anything, but faith working through love.

—GALATIANS 5:6

According to the Scriptures, the circumcision of the heart begins with water baptism (Col. 2:12). It continues to be realized through the Word of God in our lives, which is sharper than a two-edged sword, dividing asunder soul and spirit (Heb. 4:12). As we allow the Word of God to wash us and transform us, we become the circumcision, worshiping God in the spirit and having no confidence in the flesh (Phil. 3:3).

A MEMORIAL—OR MORE?

When Christ spoke to His disciples about the New Covenant that would be established through the shedding of His blood, He gave a memorial that they were to keep in remembrance of Him. We call it the *Lord's Table,* or the *Lord's Supper.*

When Jesus celebrated that last fateful Passover with His disciples, He broke the bread and gave it to the disciples, and said, "Take, eat; this is My body." When He took the cup and gave thanks, He gave it to them, saying, "Drink from it, all of you. For this is My blood of the new covenant, which is shed for many for the remission of sins" (Matt. 26:26–28). He referred to the reality of the blood covenant, with which the disciples and all Jews were familiar, in circumcision as well as in the type and shadow of animal sacrifices.

> Our change of identity can be as dramatic as Abraham's as we lose our identity and accept the identity we have in Christ Jesus through His blood covenant.

65

I always felt there must be something more in the meaning of the Lord's Table than what I understood from church tradition. For a long time I had asked the question, "What is the underlying principle involved in this memorial?" The very language of Jesus when He said, "Most assuredly, I say to you, unless you eat the flesh of the Son of Man and drink His blood, you have no life in you" (John 6:53), added to my perplexity. "What did He mean by it?" I would ask.

While we cannot accept the doctrine of transubstantiation, which teaches that when we partake of the bread and wine they become the literal body of Christ, I believe there is more reality in our celebrating the Lord's supper than much of the church has believed. The key to experiencing the reality of the Lord's table and appropriating all the wonderful provisions of Calvary to our lives is faith. Full salvation—salvation to the uttermost—was provided at Calvary. If we keep the memorial of the Lord's table as Jesus instructed us to do, we can by faith appropriate whatever need we have of His wonderful redemption.

When Abraham entered into a blood covenant with God, there were several striking changes in his life that related to that cutting of covenant. Among them was the changing of his name from *Abram* to *Abraham.* The H sound is directly related to the title for God, *Yah,* which the Hebrews used. It refers to the breath of God that touched Abraham in that awesome event. Abraham became part of the royalty of God in the cutting of covenant with God. Our change of identity can be as dramatic as Abraham's as we lose our identity and accept the identity we have in Christ Jesus through His blood covenant. Each time we memorialize that covenant, we can come into a deeper reality of who we are in Christ.

The Abrahamic covenant, the basis for Judaism and Christianity, is the most marvelous document in existence. Its seal of circumcision (Gen. 17) bound Abraham and his descendants with indescribable ties to Jehovah, and it bound Jehovah to Abraham and his descendants by the same solemn token. In effect God was saying, "My substitute has

66

been slain. I want you to circumcise yourself so the blood of my substitute will be mingled." When that was done, it meant that all Abraham had or ever would have was laid on the altar. It meant that God must sustain and protect Abraham to the limit.

Similarly, the New Testament Scriptures teach that our life is hid in God, and as Paul declared:

> I have been crucified with Christ; it is no longer I
> who live, but Christ lives in me; and the life which
> I now live in the flesh I live by faith in the Son of
> God, who loved me and gave Himself for me.
> —GALATIANS 2:20

Abraham experienced a type of death and resurrection when the glory of God appeared to him, and God cut covenant with him. His name was changed, and the eternal promises of God became His. We should note that this transforming experience did not happen at the beginning of Abraham's call from God. Abraham had already left his homeland and had separated from his nephew, Lot, because of tensions among their herdsmen. Cutting covenant that results in the promises of eternal life presupposes a total commitment to the lordship of Christ. Only then can we experience the reality of mutual commitment and enjoy the blessings of redemption and revelation of the glory of God in our lives.

67

THE BURNING BUSH

Throughout the history of mankind, God has been restoring

communion with Himself to His people. During the time of the patriarchs, He cut covenant with men to whom He chose to reveal His desire for relationship. His promises to Abraham were coming to pass through his sons and descendants. When they began to multiply as God had promised, they were living in Egypt, and became odious to the people and rulers of Egypt. They suffered during several hundred years of bondage before God appeared to Moses in the burning bush to say that He had heard the groaning of His people. It was time for their deliverance by His powerful hand.

> Now Moses kept the flock of Jethro his father in law, the priest of Midian: and he led the flock to the backside of the desert, and came to the mountain of God, even to Horeb. And the angel of the LORD appeared unto him in a flame of fire out of the midst of a bush: and he looked, and, behold, the bush burned with fire, and the bush was not consumed. And Moses said, I will now turn aside, and see this great sight, why the bush is not burnt. And when the LORD saw that he turned aside to see, God called unto him out of the midst of the bush, and said, Moses, Moses. And he said, Here am I. And he said, Draw not nigh hither: put off thy shoes from off thy feet, for the place whereon thou standest is holy ground. Moreover he said, I am the God of thy father, the God of Abraham, the God of Isaac, and the God of Jacob. And Moses hid his face; for he was afraid to look upon God.
>
> —EXODUS 3:1–6, KJV

According to historians, the heat in the desert was such that to see a bush burning in flames during the day was not uncommon. It is very probable that Moses had seen many bushes on fire in the severe heat of the desert where he lived for many years as a shepherd. The bush that Moses saw in flames on this particular day, however, was extraordinary, because it kept burning without being consumed. This caused him to turn aside and see "this great sight," to know why the bush didn't burn up. He was probably not prepared for the true greatness of the sight he was to behold.

When God saw that Moses came to see the bush, He

> If you will only respond to the presence of God, however He appears, you may receive a personal revelation of God that surprises you.

69

called to him from the midst of the bush. Such a revelation of the glory of God in that desert place was not what Moses had expected. Yet he was convinced that it was God speaking to him, and he took off his shoes because he was standing on holy ground. Though he hid his face, not daring to look on God, he did listen to the instructions he was receiving. The dialogue that followed revealed once again the longing heart of God who had determined to deliver His people from their affliction. When Moses asked God's name, He responded, "I AM THAT I AM."

Perhaps you can relate to Moses' low expectation as he

beheld an otherwise common sight—a burning bush—but one that was not consumed in the burning. Maybe you do not consider your person or your circumstances to be worthy of a sudden revelation of the glory of God. But if you will only respond to the presence of God, however He appears, you may receive a personal revelation of God that surprises you. God desires so much to reveal His glory to you that, though you cannot look on Him and live, He will find a way to communicate intimately with you.

Your response to your "burning-bush experiences" could lead you into the destiny for your life—as it did Moses—and to a fuller revelation of the glory of God. Moses received direction not only for himself, but for those God entrusted to him to be delivered from their afflictions. You should not despair over your circumstances, even when they seem as bleak as the life of Moses on the back side of the desert, for God knows your address, and He will find you as you look to Him in spite of your circumstances.

You are probably familiar with the biblical record that recounts the wonders God did as Moses obeyed the word of the Lord he received that day at the burning bush. The revelation he received there opened a dialogue between him and God that, in the days following, continued to reveal the plan of deliverance for the children of Israel one step at a time. Though it was not without its difficulties and challenges, the path for a great deliverance for God's people had been opened.

THE PASSOVER LAMB REVEALED

The Old Testament is so rich with the typology of the

revelation of the glory of God that we could write volumes if we lingered here. While we cannot do that, we must at least give some attention to the beautiful revelation of the glory of God in the Passover lamb. God instructed Moses to have the people prepare a perfect lamb, one without blemish, to exquisite detail by the instructions of the Lord. The blood of that lamb was to be sprinkled on the doorposts of every home in Israel in order for them to escape the death angel that took the life of every firstborn male in Egyptian homes. These were the instructions they received:

> Your lamb shall be without blemish, a male of the first year: ye shall take it out from the sheep, or from the goats . . . And they shall take of the blood, and strike it on the two side posts and on the upper doorpost of the houses, wherein they shall eat it. And they shall eat the flesh in that night, roast with fire, and unleavened bread; and with bitter herbs they shall eat it . . . And the blood shall be to you for a token upon the houses where ye are: and when I see the blood, I will pass over you, and the plague shall not be upon you to destroy you, when I smite the land of Egypt. And this day shall be unto you for a memorial; and ye shall keep it a feast to the LORD throughout your generations; ye shall keep it a feast by an ordinance for ever.
> —Exodus 12:5, 7–8, 13–14, KJV

71

As we discussed earlier, the hurt-love of God is represented in the typology of the Passover lamb. The Israelites were to keep as a memorial the eating of the Passover lamb every year to remind them of their deliverance from Egypt. Historically, that was a wonderfully dramatic deliverance. Yet it typified an even greater deliverance that was to be fulfilled when Christ, our Passover Lamb, gave His life for our redemption at Calvary.

Christ gave us a pattern to memorialize that ultimate sacrifice when we remember Him in the communion service. (See 1 Corinthians 11.) There is a great significance in the taking of communion that makes it more than a ritual.

We believe we can experience the presence of Christ in a powerful and intimate way as we partake of the communion elements—the bread and the wine—and receive the benefits of Calvary in faith as we remember Christ. Greater revelation of the glory of God through His wonderful redemption, along with physical healing and every provision for our well-being that were included in the sacrifice of Christ, can be appropriated as we partake in faith of the communion elements. It is sad that many Christians have forfeited this wonderful reality by allowing the communion table to become a mere ritual of tradition. Spiritual life can be renewed and strengthened as we realize what Christ intended when He commanded us to keep this memorial in His name.

THE CLOUD OF
GLORY AND PILLAR OF FIRE

When God delivered the children of Israel from Egypt, His plan involved a journey through the wilderness before they would reach the Promised Land. For that journey they would need supernatural guidance, which would involve another revelation of God's glory:

> And the LORD went before them by day in a pillar of a cloud, to lead them the way; and by night in a pillar of fire, to give them light; to go by day and night: He took not away the pillar of the cloud by day, nor the pillar of fire by night, from before the people.
>
> —EXODUS 13:21–22, KJV

The people of Israel were blessed with the supernatural guidance of God Himself as they traveled into the wilderness to make their great escape from Egypt. The well-known Bible commentator Matthew Henry explains:

> As they came to the edge of the wilderness (v. 20) they needed a guide; and a very good guide they had, one that was infinitely wise, kind and faithful. The Shekinah (or appearance of the divine Majesty, which was typical of Christ) or a previous manifestation of the eternal Word, which, in the fulness of time was to be made flesh, and dwell among us. Christ was with the church in the wilderness.
>
> Those who make the glory of God their end, and word of God their rule, the Spirit of God the guide of their affections, and the providence of God the guide of their affairs, may be confident that the Lord goes before them, as truly as he went before

73

Israel in the wilderness, though not so sensibly; we must live by faith.

They had sensible evidence of God's going before them. They all saw an appearance from heaven of a pillar, which in the bright day appeared cloudy, and in the dark night appeared fiery. God gave them this ocular demonstration of his presence, in compassion to the infirmity of their faith, and in compliance with that infant state of the church, which needed to be thus lisped to in their own language.

When they marched, this pillar went before them, at the rate that they could follow, and apointed the place of their encampment, as Infinite Wisdom saw fit, which both eased them from care, and secured them from danger, both in moving and in resting. It sheltered them by day from the heat, which, at some times of the year, was extreme. It gave them light by night when they had occasion for it, and at all times made their camp pleasant and the wilderness they were in less frightful.

Some make this cloud a type of Christ. The cloud of his human nature was a veil to the light and fire of his divine nature; we find him (Rev. 10:1) clothed with a cloud, and his feet as pillars of fire. Christ is our way, the light of our way and the guide of it.[1]

During their wilderness journey, God desired to speak to

His people further, to communicate His great heart of love and His purposes for them. After the children of Israel refused to hear from Him directly, out of fear, they asked Moses to be their mediator between them and God. God condescended once again to their request, and gave Moses the plan for God's presence to dwell with His people. It was an elaborate plan and one that is filled with beautiful types and shadows of the coming of Christ centuries later. We can only introduce here this revelation of God's glory through the tabernacle of Moses.

THE TABERNACLE OF MOSES

Moses' tabernacle was the habitation of God when the children of Israel were wandering in the wilderness from Mount Sinai to Shiloh in the Promised Land. It was constructed of boards overlaid with various curtains and coverings and consisted of three parts: the outer court, the holy place and the most holy place. In each of these respective places, God commanded certain furnishings to be set. All had to be built according to the divine standard, the pattern the Lord gave to Moses on the mount. The tabernacle was built by the enabling of the wisdom and Spirit of God.

75

The ark of the covenant was the most important piece of furniture in the tabernacle. It was the place where the manifest presence, the *shekinah glory* of God, appeared between the two cherubim on the Day of Atonement each year. All that the ark was to Israel in the Old Testament, Jesus Christ is to His church in the New Testament. God gave instructions to Moses on Mount Sinai for the construction of the ark. It was first anointed with the holy anointing oil, and then the glory of the Lord filled the tabernacle so that no man could minister by reason of that glory.

> As we behold Jesus, His presence will evoke the highest worship from our hearts, and we will be changed into His image from glory to glory.

It was here within the veil that the high priest would come and sprinkle blood upon the mercy seat once a year, on the great Day of Atonement, to make atonement for the sins of the whole nation. Christ Jesus was once and for all offered for our sins, and now we have boldness to enter into the holiest of all by His precious blood. (See Hebrews 6:18–20; 10:19–20.) Some of the most important truths represented by the ark of the covenant could be summarized as follows. The ark of God represented:

- The throne of God in the earth

- The presence of God among His redeemed people, Israel

- The glory of God revealed in divine order among His saints

- The fullness of the Godhead, bodily revealed in the Lord Jesus Christ (See Colossians 1:19; 2:9.)[2]

Within the ark there were three articles: the tables of law, the golden pot of manna and the rod of Aaron that had budded. These were symbolic of the Father's law, the Son as our heavenly manna and the fruitfulness of the Holy Spirit. They also symbolize the fullness of the Godhead bodily in the Lord Jesus Christ.

The ark took the central position in the march of Israel. Thus the presence of God was the focus of their journey to the Promised Land. For New Testament believers, the Lord Jesus Christ must be the focus of our journey into the inheritance He purchased for us at Calvary. As we behold Jesus, His presence will evoke the highest worship from our hearts, and we will be changed into His image from glory to glory.

Chapter 6

The Glory
Revealed in Worship

Human Hearts Touching God's Heart

T he glory of God revealed to our hearts is the most
powerful catalyst to worship. No one can stand in the
manifest presence of God without experiencing the
reverence and awe of a heart bowed in worship. Con-
versely, it is also true that as we choose to worship God in
spirit and in truth without sensing His manifest presence,
God chooses to reveal His glory to us in that place of
worship.

As we have seen in the life of Moses, when he encountered
the burning bush in the desert and heard the voice of God
calling to him, he worshiped there on that holy ground. Yet
again when He sought God specifically asking to see His
glory, God allowed Moses to see His goodness and mercy.
Whether it is by God's initiative or by ours, through our
choosing to worship Him, it is clear that God desires to
reveal His glory to hungry hearts. To summarize, it is our

worship that brings a revelation of His glory, and it is a revelation of His glory that brings us to worship.

THE TABERNACLE OF DAVID

God went to great lengths to reveal His plan for worship to the children of Israel, which resulted in the tabernacle and the ark of the covenant, as we have discussed. While the plan of salvation and the provision for atonement of sin was represented in type in the ark of the covenant, it was in the tabernacle of David that the revelation of worship in spirit and in truth was more completely typified. Many scholars feel that David transcended the Old Testament covenants and experienced the freedom and joy that the New Covenant of the blood of Christ would provide. In his book *The Tabernacle of David,* Kevin Conner discussed the typology of the glory of David's tabernacle, comparing it to the tabernacle of Moses. In this chapter I have adapted much of his teaching on this subject to help us better understand this typology.

> In contrast to the Tabernacle of Moses and the Priests at Mount Gibeon, these Priests in the Tabernacle at Zion did not offer animal sacrifices. They offered sacrifices of praise and joy and thanksgiving. Here the ministry of the singers and musicians was in full operation. They were to offer up "spiritual sacrifices" in Mount Zion in the Tabernacle of David.[1]

The writer to the Hebrews admonishes New Covenant Christians, "By him therefore let us offer the sacrifice of praise to God continually, that is, the fruit of our lips giving thanks to his name" (Heb. 13:15, kjv).

> Again, the Tabernacle of David had no Outer Court with its attendant furniture, no Holy Place with its attendant furniture, in contrast to the Tabernacle of Moses at Gibeon.
>
> These Priests and Levites simply had the Holiest of All, or the Most Holy Place and in it the Ark of the Covenant...
>
> In Old Testament actuality, David had *transferred* the Ark of the Covenant from the Tabernacle of Moses to the Tabernacle of David. There was simply a transference of the Holiest of All. The Priests in David's Tabernacle could simply and boldly enter into the Most Holy Place. They had access before the Ark of the Lord. There was no standing veil between them and the Ark, as there had been for centuries in the Tabernacle of Moses. They had boldness (typically) to enter in "within the veil" because that veil belonged to the Tabernacle of Moses, NOT to the Tabernacle of David.
>
> Once the dedicatory sacrifices had been offered, no more animal sacrifices were offered in David's Tabernacle, only spiritual sacrifices. What joy and praise must have been in the hearts and on the lips of those Priests and Levites who had been

81

transferred from the form of Moses' tabernacle to the glory of David's tabernacle.[2]

Bible commentators generally agree that David set up musical instruments in both places of worship—the high place of Gibeon, which was the site of Moses' tabernacle, and in Zion—the place of David's tabernacle that held the ark of the covenant. (See 1 Chronicles 16:39–43.) Up to this time no such ministry had been in Moses' tabernacle.[3]

SIGNIFICANCE OF DAVID'S TABERNACLE

That which David did typically and prophetically were fulfilled historically and actually by Jesus Christ. When Jesus died on the Cross, and God rent the veil of the Temple in twain, the Holiest of All was opened. Access was made available for all who would enter in through Christ Jesus. There was a transference of the Holiest of All, or Most Holy Place, from the Old Law Covenant Church—Israel after the flesh—to the New Covenant Church in grace—Israel after the Spirit.

The Epistle to the Hebrews clearly confirms that which took place in the Gospels. It gives us the true spiritual significance of the rent veil. The Gospels record the historical account of the rent veil, but the Epistle to the Hebrews interprets that account for us.

The Epistle to the Hebrews clearly shows us that we have access into the Holiest of All, "within the veil." No longer does the veil (literally, "that which divides") stand between us and God. No longer do we need a material earthly Tabernacle with its Outer Court and Holy Place. The Most Holy Place, the Holiest of All in a greater and more perfect Tabernacle, is now open to us. It is this glory that is typified and prophetically set forth in the Tabernacle of David...

Jews and Gentiles now have access to God in Christ (Ephesians 2:18). Access, entrance within the veil and boldness to do so is made possible by the blood of Jesus. The Priests and Levites in David's Tabernacle had this typically.

No wonder the Book of Acts says, "And a great company of the priests were obedient to the faith" (Acts 6:7, KJV). As the Gospel news spread, these Priests must have realized the futility of carrying on animal sacrifices, the Aaronic Priesthood and the Mosaic economy in a material Temple that God had finished with. Once the veil was rent in two, it was useless to carry on the form. The Lord Jesus Christ was the sacrifice. He was the True Temple. He was the Priest after the Order of Melchisedek. It is through His sacrifice, His body and blood, that all may have access to God...

The rending of the veil in connection with the Cross of Jesus shows vividly that the Holiest of All was opened then and there for all who believe, be they Jew or Gentile. Jesus Christ is the Great High Priest, and the Cross was the whole of the sacrificial

83

system compounded into one perfect sacrifice. All the sacrifices offered on the various Feast Days were compounded in that one sacrifice of Jesus. Passover and Day of Atonement were united in the Cross, as far as the body and blood sacrifice of Jesus was concerned. This is why He could enter "within the veil" and why we also have boldness to enter in after our forerunner. He was both Priest and sacrifice because of the union in His person of the Divine and human natures.[4]

Here was worship perfected in the eyes of the Father.

JOY AND REJOICING IN WORSHIP

The glory of God that dwelt with His people in these Old Testament tabernacles and temples had chosen to become *incarnate* in the Son of God so that we could more perfectly relate to the glory of God. (See chapter 7.) Through our relationship with Christ in the new birth, we become temples for the glory of God. (See chapter 8.) Simply defined, a *temple* is a place of worship where God and His beloved can commune together. This awesome love relationship can hardly be explained. As the country preacher once exclaimed, "It is better felt than telt."

When David and all Israel brought the ark of the covenant back to Jerusalem from its place of captivity, they did it with great joy and rejoicing. The Scriptures declare that King David laid aside his royal robes and, clothed in a linen ephod, danced with all his might before the ark of the Lord.

There is no adequate expression for experiencing the glory of God. It simply requires all our might and strength to release the joy and rejoicing that consume our beings when the glory of God touches our hearts.

Worship is the appropriate response to the glory of God. Joy and rejoicing are the pervading emotions of worship—the highest human expression of adoration to God. It is a result of knowing that God has defeated our enemies, who were too strong for us. After God told Jehoshaphat to "stand still and see the salvation of the LORD," the people witnessed the hand of God setting ambushes and slaying the armies that had come against them (2 Chron. 20:17, 22–23). Then the people picked up the riches left by the defeated armies and "returned, every man of Judah and Jerusalem...to go back to Jerusalem with joy, for the LORD had made them rejoice over their enemies" (v. 27). They went into the house of the Lord with musical instruments and celebrated the victory God had given them.

> Through our relationship with Christ in the new birth, we become temples for the glory of God.

85

REVERENCE IN WORSHIP

While joy and rejoicing may be the outward response to the presence of God, the glory of God revealed to us will work a deep reverence in our hearts toward God. Again, the writer to the Hebrews communicated this truth, declaring:

> Therefore, since we receive a kingdom which can-
> not be shaken, let us show gratitude, by which we
> may offer to God an acceptable service with rever-
> ence and awe; for our God is a consuming fire.
> —HEBREWS 12:28–29, NAS

Gratitude to God should be the motivating force by which we offer our acceptable service, with reverence. In the New Testament, the Greek word *aidos* is translated as "rever-ence." It means "awe and godly fear." The heart of a wor-shiper is one that is truly grateful for the goodness of God to redeem, forgive, heal and restore our broken lives to intimate relationship with Him. Gratitude for "so great a salvation" evokes reverence—awe and godly fear—from sinful creatures who are being redeemed from their sin.

True reverence for God involves living a reverent life—not just acting reverent in church. Serving God with reverence means showing Him honor and respect in every area of our lives. We understand that God has come to earth in Christ and that Christ dwells in our hearts by the Holy Spirit. A gen-uine revelation of this reality changes our attitude toward all of life. We learn to revere the presence of God that lives in us, whether we are sitting in a restaurant, doing the dishes, driving our car or engaging in casual conversation.

If Christ is truly King in our lives, reverence for Him will be seen in our submission to His lordship in the decisions that gov-ern our daily lives. How do we show reverence? Is it by the way we sing? Pray? By our silence? Is it confined to some particular tradition or form of worship? If we are cultivating a grateful heart, we will exhibit a reverent attitude in every aspect of our lives. We will continually become more sensitive to irreverent speech and unkind attitudes that do not bring glory to God.

We need to understand that reverence and respect are expressions of love. To respect and revere God is to love Him. And to love Him is to obey Him. The glory of God will be revealed through our lives as we reverence Him always. Worship will be motivated by true reverence for God. Cultivating reverence for God will bring us into new realms of worship. As we learn to walk in awe and godly fear, we will come to the revelation of the psalmist: "Be still, and know that I am God" (Ps. 46:10). There is a place of deep awe and reverence for the majesty of who God is, where all we can do is wait in silence before Him.

> Worship is the appropriate response to the glory of God. Joy and rejoicing are the pervading emotions of worship—the highest human expression of adoration to God.

87

In the tabernacle of Moses, when the priest entered the holy of holies once a year, he witnessed the manifest presence—the glory—of God. He did not respond in dancing or rejoicing. In that place there was such awe and reverence that it evoked a deep silence. Having said that, joy and rejoicing are natural responses to the presence of God. We hasten to add that often the glory of His presence will evoke such awe and reverence that we can only respond in deep silence. We will touch realms of worship where we wait silently in God's presence and allow Him to touch our lives in a deep and reverential way.

FELLOWSHIP IN WORSHIP

The deepest longing of the human heart is spiritual. Because mankind was made for fellowship with God, our soul cries out for that divine relationship, even if we are not aware of what it should be. We suffer a kind of cosmic loneliness without the attachment to God that He ordained we should enjoy. Only as we become bearers of His glory can we hope to find true fulfillment.

The divine longing for relationship with God implies that the soul has a capacity for greatness. Linking the finite with the infinite—the human soul with the heart of God—opens us to true greatness through divine relationship. That relationship alone can satisfy the deepest longing of the human heart. Possessions, position, even ideal family relationships cannot bring us to the true satisfaction and greatness that we are destined for in God.

Every human spirit longs for fellowship with deity. We desire intimate knowledge of the Supreme Being—God Himself. And we feel an overwhelming need to be known by Him. We will never find our emotional home until we learn to walk with God. We cannot expect to be truly happy until we discover the happiness of fellowship with God. Our inner cry for divine fellowship will not be satisfied until we have learned to relate to God so intimately that we have exchanged our thoughts, feelings and decisions for God's mind, emotions and will. (See chapter 8, "Glory in Temples of Clay.")

The psalmist had come to grips with this innate desire for God, as he expresses so beautifully:

> One thing I have asked from the LORD, that I shall seek:
> That I may dwell in the house of the LORD all the days of my life,
> To behold the beauty of the LORD,
> And to meditate in His temple.
>
> —PSALM 27:4, NAS

David had developed such a relationship with God that he had only one desire, one petition for God to answer, and that was to worship God and enjoy fellowship with Him all the days of his life. In Psalm 27 he goes on to tell us how he came to that conclusion. He had discovered that God would hide him in the day of trouble, give him victory over his enemies and be a father and mother to him (vv. 5–6, 10). His heart was filled with joy because of this relationship with God, and he vowed to sing his praises to the Lord (v. 6).

> It is the seeking heart that will enjoy fellowship with God.

89

BECOME A SEEKER OF HIS PRESENCE

David gives us a secret for enjoying divine fellowship: "When Thou didst say, 'Seek My face,' my heart said to Thee, 'Thy face, O Lord, I shall seek'" (v. 8, NAS). He ends the psalm with this admonishment:

> Wait for the Lord;
> Be strong, and let your heart take courage;
> Yes, wait for the Lord.
>
> —PSALM 27:14, NAS

It is the seeking heart that will enjoy fellowship with God. We have to choose whether we will focus on lesser desires or whether we will discover the deepest longing of our hearts and be motivated to its fulfillment in God.

Do we really want to have fellowship with God? Are we pursuing the longing of our souls for relationship with Him? For His glory? If so, other desires will take a lesser place, and our lifestyle will reflect that goal. To enjoy relationship with God will necessarily limit other pursuits, no matter how noble. We have to decide if we want to pursue the deepest desire of our hearts—to know God. Of course, we will still have to make a living, nurture family relationships and perhaps pursue a career. But as we pursue relationship with God, these other pursuits will not be the focus of our energies or consume all our time. We will prioritize our lives so that we can seek God with our whole hearts. As we do, we will learn to cry with David, "Teach me Your way, O Lord, and lead me in a smooth path" (Ps. 27:11).

Too often Christians are double-minded in seeking God. We want Him, but we want other things, too. Other desires compete with our desire for God in such a way that they sometimes eclipse our seeking God. Wanting Him more than anything else involves our surrender of all other desires to His lordship. As we give ourselves to this lifelong process of surrender, we will be delighted with our discovery of His desires for us. Walking in the blessing of the Lord, communing with Him and knowing we are fulfilling His purpose for our lives is so satisfying that it makes all our natural desires pale by comparison.

The Shulamite girl described in the Song of Solomon (or Song of Songs) at one time suffered a halfhearted desire for her beloved:

> **If we want to experience the glory of God in our lives continually, we will always need to be seekers of His presence.**

91

> On my bed night after night I sought him
> Whom my soul loves;
> I sought him but did not find him.
> I must arise now and go about the city;
> In the streets and in the squares
> I must seek him whom my soul loves.
> —SONG OF SOLOMON 3:1–2, NAS

She was accustomed to having her lover with her in the comfort of her surroundings. She had limited her seeking of him to a place where she had found him once—upon her bed.

This bed is a picture of her indolence, of her wanting her

beloved on her own terms or at least on the same comfortable terms she had once known. Night after night she was willing to be without his presence unless he came to her as he had done before. Finally, when he did not come, she decided she had to go and seek him where he was. When she made the effort to go out into the city, she found him again and would not let him go (v. 4). She had to get out of her comfort zone—her own pattern, ideas and customary ways of seeking him. Finding him required effort on her part and an intensity that would not let her give up until she had accomplished her goal.

We can learn an important lesson from her experience. If we want to experience the glory of God in our lives continually, we will always need to be seekers of His presence. Have we experienced the presence of God in certain places or through particular devotional and worship patterns? Are we expecting always to find our Beloved there? If we are sensing a lack of His presence, it may be that He wants us to seek Him in new ways or with greater intensity. Seeking Him reveals our true desire for His glory. Perhaps He hides Himself simply so that He can take delight in our desire for Him.

92

Many people are comfortable with religious creeds and traditions of worship, but they do not want to know God personally. They live their lives for themselves and acknowledge God only on Sunday when they repeat prayers they have learned and sing the hymns of the church. In any church tradition it is possible to learn the format of the religious services without choosing in our hearts to become deeply involved in seeking the presence of God for our lives. Unless we do, we cannot hope to know the revelation of His glory to our hearts.

May we be like Simeon the priest and Anna of old who lived

in the temple and waited with hope for the revelation of the glory of God, the Prince of Peace, the Savior who had been promised. The incarnate Lord would not disappoint those who truly desired to see Him and sought for Him all their lives. They would behold His glory, while others who saw Him as an infant failed to recognize Him as the King of kings.

Chapter 7

The Glory Incarnate

The Word Made Flesh

So sacred is the subject to which we now turn that we sense a desire to "take off our shoes because we stand on holy ground." The loving heart of God that we have seen throughout the history of mankind, reaching out to lost humanity with intense desire to reveal His glory to us, has now reached the apex of intensity. And in the fullness of time, having laid the foundation throughout the biblical types and shadows, the historical narrative and the prophetic voices, God Himself became man in order to perfectly redeem mankind to Himself.

> And the Word became flesh, and dwelt among us, and we beheld His glory, glory as of the only begotten from the Father, full of grace and truth.
> —JOHN 1:14, NAS

The Incarnation—God becoming man—is merely a vague

theological premise to our minds unless we can meditate on the wonder of it and allow the Holy Spirit to unveil its overwhelming significance to our hearts and minds. If we are to experience the glory of God revealed through our lives, we must relate properly to the incarnate glory of God manifested in Jesus Christ. Speaking of Christ, the writer to the Hebrews declares:

> God, after He spoke long ago to the fathers in the prophets in many portions and in many ways, in these last days has spoken to us in His Son, whom He appointed heir of all things, through whom also He made the world. And He is the radiance of His glory and the exact representation of His nature, and upholds all things by the word of His power. When He had made purification of sins, He sat down at the right hand of the Majesty on high.
> —HEBREWS 1:1–3, NAS

The incarnation of Christ is the ultimate act of God to reveal His glory to mankind. He perfectly represents the nature of God and is the radiance of His glory. Lewis Sperry Chafer correctly places the Incarnation as one of the seven greatest events that have occurred in the history of the universe:

1. The creation of the angels
2. Creation of material things, including all life on the earth
3. The incarnation
4. The death of the Incarnate One

5. His resurrection
6. His coming again
7. His reign on the earth forever[1]

That God in the Person of the Son should identify Himself completely with the human race, become a kinsman of the human family and as the Kinsman-Redeemer lay down His life for their redemption from sin as in the Book of Ruth, is in itself an event of immeasurable importance.[2] In my book *The Prophetic Romance,* I share how the typology of the redemption of the church is hidden in this wonderful Old Testament allegory.

In the Book of Ruth, Boaz, the kinsman-redeemer, prefigures Christ who was willing to lay down His life to redeem His bride. This historical love story demonstrates the predetermined plan of redemption that God was unfolding throughout history. Boaz acted according to the Law of Moses given to the children of Israel by God, which made provision for the redemption of the poor. It stated that if someone became so poor that he could not pay his debts, he could sell his land and/or himself to pay his debtors. How much he sold depended on the extent of his debt. Even after he was sold, however, he retained a right of redemption (Lev. 25:48–54).

There were three ways, according to the Law, that a man who had succumbed to poverty could redeem himself and his land. First, if he could accumulate enough to buy back his land, he was free to do so (Lev. 25:26–27, 49–50). Second, if he could not buy back his land, he would have to work as a hired hand until the year of Jubilee, celebrated every fifty years. At that time all property was returned to its original owner and all who had sold themselves and their property could return to their land (Lev. 25:28, 54). How anxiously everyone awaited the Jubilee when all mortgages were canceled and those who had succumbed to poverty were given a second chance!

> For us to enjoy our complete restoration in Christ, we have only to choose to turn our feet toward the place provided for our redemption, continually yielding our lives to His plan for us.

The third way a man could be redeemed was if one of his brothers or another blood relative would purchase what his indebted relative had sold (Lev. 25:47–53). According to this law, it was the responsibility of a near kinsman to come and buy back what his relative had sold (Lev. 25:25). In the story of Ruth, Boaz indicates this fact by stating there is a nearer kinsman than he, to whom he is obligated to appeal before offering redemption to Ruth. In the case of a widow who had no son to care for her, it became the responsibility of the brother of the deceased husband to marry her, redeem her lost inheritance and raise up seed for his brother's house (Deut. 25:5–10). For the Israelites, these laws could not be treated as mere suggestions for proper conduct. If they were not strictly obeyed, those who violated them would have consequences to pay.

Naomi was both a victim of poverty and of the loss of her husband and sons. The laws of redemption we have described made provision for a widow in Israel. Though her plight seemed desperate, Naomi knew there was a means of redemption provided for her according to the Law of Moses. In type, these laws foreshadow the wonderful, eternal redemption that the incarnate Christ has provided for His church.

The church has not been bought with silver or gold, but with the precious blood of the incarnate Christ who made atonement for our sins. Through His sacrifice at Calvary, God has redeemed us from the curse of sin with its death and destruction. Because of Adam and Eve's disobedience to God's command, they were separated from relationship with God. As a result of that separation, they not only lost their innocence, but they also lost the privilege of maturing in the character of God. They never realized the purpose of God for mankind—to become sons of God bearing His glory.

Naomi and Ruth's story is not one of happenstance or good fortune. Centuries earlier, God had provided for their redemption in the covenant He gave to Moses. God made provision for their redemption before their birth so that when they acknowledged their need to be redeemed, they could enter into His provision. Literally, they entered into that wonderful provision. Allegorically, they showed how that provision was available to the church.

Redemption was provided long before our birth. The Scriptures teach that Christ was the Lamb slain from the foundation of the world (Rev. 13:8). Though there was a specific moment in history when Jesus came to earth as the incarnate Son of God to fulfill the plan of redemption, He was in readiness to fulfill that plan for all eternity. All who lived before Christ looked forward to the provision of the cross, and we

99

who live after Christ's sacrifice on Calvary look back to that provision for our salvation. For us to enjoy our complete restoration in Christ, we have only to choose, as Naomi and Ruth did, to turn our feet toward the place provided for our redemption, continually yielding our lives to His plan for us.[3]

THE DOCTRINE
OF THE INCARNATION

The Scriptures establish the doctrine of the Incarnation in several ways:

- In the Old Testament prophecies, which represent Christ as a person both human and divine, He is set forth in "the seed" of the woman, a descendant of Abraham, of Judah and of David, "a man of sorrows." But He is also called "the Mighty God," "the Eternal Father," "the Son of God," "the Lord [Jehovah] our righteousness." Although these familiar Scriptures do not formally state the doctrine of the Incarnation, they logically suggest or lead up to it.

- In the New Testament there are many passages that present the elements of this doctrine separately— Christ is represented as a man with a human body and a rational human soul; physically and mentally He is truly human. The designation "the Son of man" occurs more than eighty times in the Gospels. But elsewhere this same person claims for Himself, and has ascribed to Him, the attributes of deity.

◍ There are numerous instances in which these two elements of Christ's personality are combined in the statement, or in which they are brought without hesitation or reserve close together (e.g., Matt. 16:27; 22:42–45; 25:31–46; Mark 14:60–62; Luke 9:43–44; John 3:31; Rom. 5:15, 21; 1 Cor. 15:47).

◍ Although the doctrine of the Incarnation does not rest upon isolated proof texts for its authority, but rather upon the Scripture revelation as a whole, still there are certain utterances of great weight in which the truth is distinctly and, we may say even formally, stated. (See John 1:1–14; cf. 1 John 1:1–3; 4:2–3; Romans 1:2–5; Philippians 2:6–11; 1 Timothy 3:16; Hebrews 2:14.) The only way in which the force of these teachings can be set aside or lessened is by proving lack of authority on the part of the Scriptures. It should be added that the only way in which the Scriptures can be understood or intelligently interpreted is in the light of the essential facts of the Incarnation.[4]

Incarnation, a theological term for the coming of God's Son into the world as a human being, itself is not used in the Bible, but it is based on clear references in the New Testament to Jesus as a person "in the flesh." (See Romans 8:3; Ephesians 2:15; Colossians 1:22.) Jesus participated fully in all that it means to live a human life. But if Jesus were merely a man, no matter how great, there would be no significance in drawing attention to His bodily existence. The marvelous thing is that in Jesus, God Himself began to live a fully human life. As the apostle Paul declared, "In Him dwells all the fullness of the Godhead bodily" (Col. 2:9). The capacity of Jesus to reveal God to us and to bring salvation depends upon His being fully God and fully man at the same time.

Our human minds cannot understand how Jesus can be both fully God and fully man. But the Bible gives clear indication of how this works out in practice.

- No person may see God and live—Exodus 33:20

- He dwells in unapproachable light—1 Timothy 6:16

- Can we, therefore, only know Him from a distance? No! God has come near in the person of Jesus—Matthew 1:23

- He has taken on a form in which He can be seen, experienced and understood by us as human beings—John 1:14, 18

- Jesus reveals God to us perfectly since, in His human life, He is the image of God—2 Corinthians 4:4

- Jesus exhibits full likeness with the Father—John 1:14

Jesus' "Godhood" in His manhood is the key to our intimate knowledge of God. This does not mean, however, that Jesus' humanity is only a display case for His divinity. Jesus lived out His human life by experiencing all the pressures, temptations and limitations that we experience (Heb. 2:18;

4:15; 5:2, 7–8). That is why Jesus' life really is the supreme human success story (Heb. 5:8). Jesus was a pioneer (Heb. 2:10, RSV), showing in practical terms the full meaning and possibility of human life lived in obedience to God. In this respect, Jesus is a kind of second Adam (Rom. 5:14–15), marking a new beginning for the human race.

Jesus would have performed a great work if He had done no more than set a perfect example. But His full humanity is also the basis on which it is possible for Him to represent us— indeed, take our place—in dying for us. The Bible makes this clear when it speaks of "one God and one Mediator between God and men, the Man Christ Jesus, who gave Himself a ransom for all" (1 Tim. 2:5–6).

When He ascended to His Father after His resurrection, Jesus left behind some of the human restrictions experienced during His earthly life. He received at that time His original divine glory (John 17:5). But the joining together of deity and humanity that marks His Incarnation did not come to an end with His ascension. Jesus took His resurrected body with Him back to heaven (Luke 24:51; Acts 1:9). In heaven now He is our divine Lord, our human leader and the great High Priest who serves as a mediator between God and man (Heb. 3:1).[5]

THE SIGNIFICANCE
OF THE INCARNATION

As we have discussed, God is ever trying to reveal Himself to mankind in order to bring us back to the original intent of His loving heart, which is that we become bearers of the nature or glory of God. Only then will we fulfill the eternal purposes of God for humanity and enjoy true satisfaction of eternal life, which He intended.

We can hope to have insight concerning God only according to the ways God has chosen to reveal Himself to us. Referring again to the Hebrews passage, the Scriptures declare:

> God, who at various times and in various ways spoke in time past to the fathers by the prophets, has in these last days spoken to us by His Son, whom He has appointed heir of all things, through whom also He made the worlds.
>
> —HEBREWS 1:1–2

This passage clearly shows us that God's way of revealing Himself to mankind, after the time of the prophets, was through His incarnate Son, Jesus Christ, who perfectly revealed God the Father. That same passage in Hebrews declares that Jesus is the "brightness of His glory and the express image of His person" (Heb. 1:3). Jesus reinforced this truth when He said to His questioning disciples, "He who has seen Me has seen the Father" (John 14:9).

Do you see progression here in the revelation of God to man? The Father is revealed to us by the Son, and the Son is revealed to us by the Holy Spirit. G. Campbell Morgan states this truth in an interesting way. He refers to Jesus as the revelation of the Father and calls the Holy Spirit the "interpretation of the revelation."[6] Although the Godhead is one Triune God, each member has His particular place and function regarding redemption as revealed in the Scriptures. Jesus said of the Holy Spirit:

> However, when He, the Spirit of truth, has come, He will guide you into all truth; for He will not speak on His own authority, but whatever He hears He will speak; and He will tell you things to come. He will glorify Me, for He will take of what is Mine and declare it to you. All things that the Father has are Mine. Therefore I said that He will take of Mine and declare it to you.
> —JOHN 16:13–15

According to this passage, the Holy Spirit did not come to minister only to the sin question. Jesus continued to declare to His disciples the work of the Holy Spirit, describing Him as *the Spirit of truth.* In order to understand the work of the Holy Spirit in our lives, we need to understand the relationship of the Holy Spirit to the incarnate Christ as He walked this earth. This will help us to understand how we can allow the Holy Spirit to reveal Christ in us as the apostle Paul declared: "Christ in you, the hope of glory" (Col. 1:27).

THE HOLY SPIRIT IN CHRIST

We have discussed the hurt-love of God that suffered the *kenosis*—the divine emptying—to become the Son of Man. The apostle Paul gives us a clear picture of the humbling of Christ to become a man, a servant of men, and the humbling of Himself ultimately to suffer death on the cross:

105

> Let this mind be in you which was also in Christ Jesus, who, being in the form of God, did not consider it robbery to be equal with God, but made Himself of no reputation, taking the form of a bondservant, and coming in the likeness of men. And being found in appearance as a man, He humbled Himself and became obedient to the point of death, even the death of the cross.
>
> — PHILIPPIANS 2:5–8

There is a sense in the Greek word *kenosis* that can be explained as the divine Son of God "parking" His deity—laying it aside—so as not to draw on the supernatural powers of His divinity as He walked the earth as a man. It is important to understand this so that we realize that Christ walked in complete dependency on the empowering of the Holy Spirit while He was on earth to accomplish His ministry and to fulfill all the will of God for redemption. Though He was God, He walked as a man filled with the Spirit of God, having emptied Himself of His divine powers in order to fulfill the Father's will of redemption for all mankind.

Jesus said:

> The Spirit of the LORD is upon me, because He anointed Me to preach the gospel to the poor. He has sent Me to proclaim release to the captives, and recovery of sight to the blind, to set free those who are downtrodden, to proclaim the favorable year of the Lord.
>
> —LUKE 4:18–19, NAS

Jesus also declared:

> I can do nothing on My own initiative. As I hear, I judge; and My judgment is just, because I do not seek My own will, but the will of Him who sent Me.
> —JOHN 5:30, NAS

Because Jesus walked in utter dependency on the Holy Spirit, He can ask us to do the same in order to manifest the glory of God through our lives. It is important that Christians understand this reality, that we do not look at Jesus' victorious life and say, "Yes, but He was God." In living life as a man, Jesus taught us that the source of victory is being filled with, empowered by and obedient to the Holy Spirit at every moment.

In order for us to understand the integral relationship of the Holy Spirit to the person and ministry of the incarnate Christ, it will help to trace the work of the Holy Spirit in the life of Jesus. This relationship is especially significant as it pertains to the humanity of Jesus. The Holy Spirit has little to do with the deity of our Lord, for Jesus was God Himself. As John so clearly declares, "In the beginning was the Word, and the

> Christ did not have His beginning in the manger in Bethlehem. He existed from all eternity—and before eternity, back in the eons of the ages before time began.

107

Word was with God, and the Word was God" (John 1:1). It is as Christ humbled Himself in the *kenosis* to bring the plan of redemption to mankind that we see the work of the Holy Spirit in His life.

IN HIS BIRTH

Of course, we understand that Christ did not have His beginning in the manger in Bethlehem. He existed from all eternity—and before eternity, back in the eons of the ages before time began. He who always existed was sent by the Spirit into the world (Isa. 48:16). It was the Holy Spirit who facilitated His coming, for Jesus was conceived by the Holy Spirit. When the angel of the Lord appeared to Mary, he declared, "The Holy Spirit will come upon you, and the power of the Highest will overshadow you; therefore, also, that Holy One who is to be born will be called the Son of God" (Luke 1:35). Then the angel of the Lord appeared to Joseph, her husband-to-be, saying, "Joseph, son of David, do not be afraid to take to you Mary your wife, for that which is conceived in her is of the Holy Spirit" (Matt. 1:20).

The divine conception of the Lord Jesus did not involve calling a new being into life as when other human beings are born. This divine One had existed eternally. Through His conception He was now entering into relationship with mankind as a human being with a human nature. He was not conceived in sin, for His conception was holy, wrought by the Holy Spirit. Without the Holy Spirit, even the incarnation of Jesus through conception would not have been possible. Likewise in our regeneration, our new birth is impossible without the Holy Spirit creating the life of God in us.

HIS PRESENTATION AT THE TEMPLE

Mary and Joseph took Jesus to Jerusalem to present Him at the temple, fulfilling the Law by offering the sacrifice required for a firstborn male (Luke 2:23). There was an old priest there named Simeon who had served God devoutly. He prayed that he not die until he see the salvation of God: "And it had been revealed to him by the Holy Spirit that he would not see death before he had seen the Lord's Christ" (Luke 2:26). The Scriptures say that Simeon went into the temple "by the Spirit" on the day that Mary and Joseph took Jesus to present Him according to the Law.

> As we allow ourselves to be filled with the Holy Spirit, we have the same possibility of victory as Jesus, who conquered the devil through the power of the Holy Spirit.

The Holy Spirit revealed to Simeon that this baby was indeed the Christ for whom he had been waiting. This godly priest began to prophesy over Jesus, to the amazement of His parents. Then Simeon declared that he was ready to die, for he had seen the salvation of God.

The Holy Spirit also included Anna, the prophetess, in this revelation of Jesus' coming. She had served God night and day with fastings and prayers, and He revealed to her that this babe was the long-awaited Savior. She began to give thanks to God and to tell everyone who was looking for the

109

redemption that Jesus, the Christ, had indeed come (Luke 2:36–38). Perhaps the revelation of the glory of God in Jesus to these two is more striking because of its contrast to all those who did not recognize His coming. Only those who knew God by the Spirit enjoyed this initial revelation.

HIS GROWTH AND MATURITY

In the Incarnation, Jesus was not created as an adult like the first Adam. He grew and developed as any other child grows, except that He did not possess any of the detriments of a sinful nature. Luke tells us, "And the Child grew and became strong in spirit, filled with wisdom; and the grace of God was upon Him" (Luke 2:40). Jesus grew into a beautiful young man filled with such wisdom that He astonished the temple rabbis of Jerusalem when He was only twelve years old. He was hearing them and asking them questions, and "all who heard Him were astonished at His understanding and answers" (Luke 2:47). Jesus' understanding of the Scriptures was not just a result of childhood studies common to Jewish boys, but was the result of the work of the Holy Spirit in Him. Isaiah's prophecy hundreds of years earlier began to be fulfilled when the boy Jesus was in the temple that day, though it would be realized in its fullest sense after His baptism. Isaiah prophesied:

> There shall come forth a Rod from the stem of Jesse, and a Branch shall grow out of his roots. The Spirit of the LORD shall rest upon Him, the Spirit of wisdom and understanding, the Spirit of counsel and might, the Spirit of knowledge and of

the fear of the LORD. His delight is in the fear of the LORD...

—ISAIAH 11:1–3

In His humanity, Jesus developed and increased in His abilities by the power of the Holy Spirit. In that same way, the glory of God—His divine nature—is developed in us as we yield to the work of the Holy Spirit to teach us the wisdom of God.

HIS BAPTISM

John the Baptist was baptizing people in the Jordan when he looked up and saw Jesus coming to him to be baptized. Although John did not feel worthy to baptize the Lamb of God, Jesus said to him, "Permit it to be so now, for thus it is fitting for us to fulfill all righteousness" (Matt. 3:15). When John baptized Jesus, the Spirit of God descended like a dove and lighted upon Him. A voice from heaven confirmed that Jesus was His beloved Son in whom the Father was well pleased (Matt. 3:16–17). The

> The Holy Spirit has come to reveal the life of our precious Lord Jesus *to us, in us* and *through us.* As He does this precious three-fold work, Christ will be able to live His life in us and reveal the glory of God through us.

111

Holy Spirit was equipping Jesus, in His baptism, for His earthly ministry, which was to follow. But first, He led Him into the wilderness to be tempted by the devil.

HIS TEMPTATION

The Scriptures clearly indicate that the Holy Spirit not only led Christ into the wilderness, but that all the time Christ was there the Holy Spirit was with Him, enabling Him to overcome the severe temptations of the evil one (Matt. 4:1). Luke tells us that Jesus was full of the Holy Ghost when He was led by the Spirit into the wilderness (Luke 4:1). By the power of the Holy Spirit, Jesus' human nature was given the strength to withstand the enemy and to overcome the severe temptations placed before Him. His victory was not because of the qualities of His divine nature being infused into His human nature, for then He would no longer have been a man. Being a complete man, He relied only on the indwelling Holy Spirit for His ability to resist the temptations of the evil one. When He had conquered temptations of the devil by declaring, "It is written," Luke tells us He "returned in the power of the Spirit to Galilee" (Luke 4:14).

We know that Jesus was not cornered by the devil. He was led out, or as Mark said, *driven* by the Spirit into the wilderness to meet the enemy (Mark 1:12). This can be very instructive for believers who find themselves in a place of testing or temptation. The Christian who is subject to temptation or personal testing is not necessarily out of the will of God. There are times in life that we must face the tempter, as Jesus did, with a clear response: "It is written." As we allow ourselves to be filled with the Holy Spirit, we have the same possibility of victory as Jesus, who conquered the devil through the power of the Holy Spirit.

HIS MINISTRY

The Holy Spirit anointed Jesus with power for His earthly ministry, as we have mentioned. Jesus Himself attributed His works to the divine anointing of the Holy Spirit who worked through Him when He stood in the temple and read from the prophet Isaiah (Luke 4:18–19). Peter also preached this truth to the house of Cornelius, telling them that "God anointed Jesus of Nazareth with the Holy Spirit and with power, who went about doing good and healing all who were oppressed by the devil, for God was with Him" (Acts 10:38).

It was through the divine power of the Holy Spirit that Jesus could do miracles. The Pharisees had accused Jesus of casting out demons by the power of Beelzebub, the prince of demons. But Jesus showed them the foolishness of thinking that Satan would cast out himself. Then He instructed them that if He "cast out demons by the Spirit of God, surely the kingdom of God has come upon you" (Matt. 12:28). His ministry was performed by the power of the Holy Spirit who is also resident within us today as Spirit-filled believers.

113

HIS TRANSFIGURATION

> Jesus took Peter, James, and John his brother, led them up on a high mountain by themselves; and He was transfigured before them. His face shone like the sun, and His clothes became as white as the light.
>
> —MATTHEW 17:1–2

When Jesus was transfigured before His disciples, the unveiling of the glory of God that was in Him was seen in His human vessel. That unveiling was done by the blessed Holy Spirit. How awesome that the manifested presence of the glory of the infinite God was seen for a few moments by the disciples! Is it any wonder that Peter wanted to build three tabernacles?

I believe God is going to take the church to the Mount of Transfiguration and reveal the glory of God in her to the world. (See chapter 10—"Glory in the Church.") Jesus prayed for His disciples in His high priestly prayer:

> And the glory which You gave Me I have given them, that they may be one just as We are one…Father, I desire that they also whom You gave Me may be with Me where I am, that they may behold My glory which You have given Me.
>
> —JOHN 17:22, 24

Returning to our definition of the glory of God, we understand that the nature of the Father and of Christ, the divine attributes of God, reveal His glory. That glory is going to shine through the lives of His people. As we learn to yield completely to the Holy Spirit, He will perfect the life and character of God within us and reveal it to the world.

HIS DEATH

It was not enough that Jesus suffer and die for our sins; He had to do so in the proper manner. Abraham Kuyper expresses this fact so clearly:

Christ did not redeem us by His suffering alone, being spit upon, scourged, crowned with thorns, crucified, slain. This passion was made effectual to our redemption by His love and voluntary obedience. Hence there was in Christ's suffering much more than mere passive penal satisfaction. Nobody compelled Christ. He who partook of the divine nature could not be compelled but offered Himself voluntarily. "Lo I come to do thy will, Oh God, in the volume of the Book it is written of Me."[7]

Jesus was empowered and enabled by the Holy Spirit to offer this acceptable sacrifice for the sins of the whole world. The perfection of Christ's sacrifice in His obedient, loving attitude was made possible by the eternal Spirit of God (Heb. 9:14). Without the enabling of the Holy Spirit, the Man, Jesus, could not have offered Himself a perfect sacrifice to God.

115

HIS RESURRECTION

Sometimes the resurrection of Jesus is attributed to the Father (Acts 2:24). Other times it is said to be the work of the Son Himself (John 10:17–18). But the resurrection is also in a special way the work of the Holy Spirit. Paul writes:

> But if the Spirit of Him who raised Jesus from the dead dwells in you, He who raised Christ from the dead will also give life to your mortal bodies through His Spirit who dwells in you.
> —ROMANS 8:11

The Spirit of God working with the Father gave resurrection

life to Jesus. He still offers that same resurrection life to every believer who will receive from His hand the things of Jesus.

We cannot continue here the discussion of the work of the Holy Spirit through Jesus in the birthing of the church, the baptizing of the church and in progressive sanctification.[8] However, we can conclude from this brief synopsis that the Holy Spirit has come to reveal the life of our precious Lord Jesus *to us, in us* and *through us.* As He does this precious threefold work, Christ will be able to live His life in us and reveal the glory of God through us. For this reason Paul declared boldly: "Christ in you, the hope of glory" (Col. 1:27).

The life of the incarnate Christ dwelling in a finite human being is almost incomprehensible. Faith is required to grasp the significance of the Incarnation of God in Christ to my personal life. And God Himself supplies that faith, as the Scriptures declare:

> For by grace are ye saved through faith; and that not of yourselves: it is the gift of God:
> —EPHESIANS 2:8, KJV

The apostle Paul had learned his complete dependency on the Holy Spirit for his very life, declaring:

> I am crucified with Christ: nevertheless I live; yet not I, but Christ liveth in me: and the life which I now live in the flesh I live by the faith of the Son of God, who loved me, and gave himself for me.
> —GALATIANS 2:20, KJV

Our union with Christ determines how perfectly we will reflect the glory of God in our lives. We should be encouraged to yield ourselves completely to the Holy Spirit who will enable us to be changed into the image of the incarnate Christ and become bearers of the glory of God in the earth.

Chapter 8

Glory in Temples of Clay

The Holy Spirit Brings the Glory

Though it is incredible to understand that God became man in the Incarnation, it may be even more incredible to understand that God has chosen to place His divine life inside human vessels when we are born again by the power of the Holy Spirit. The Scriptures declare that in salvation we are "born again, not of corruptible seed, but of incorruptible, by the word of God, which liveth and abideth for ever" (1 Pet. 1:23, KJV). That divine life of God lives in our spirit, making us sons of God.

To think that we become a part of the family of God when we are born again is one of the most wonderful realizations the human heart can experience. This eternal reality caused the apostle Peter to exclaim:

> Of this salvation the prophets have inquired and searched carefully, who prophesied of the grace

that would come to you...To them it was revealed that, not to themselves, but to us they were ministering the things which now have been reported to you through those who have preached the gospel to you by the Holy Spirit sent from heaven—things which angels desire to look into.

—1 PETER 1:10, 12

It seems that even angelic beings in heaven cannot fully understand the wonder of so great a salvation as we receive when we are born again. The Scriptures show us that this salvation will be the theme of praise and worship throughout all eternity, as we express our deep gratitude and adoration for the Lamb of God who made our redemption possible. When John saw into heaven he heard a "loud voice saying in heaven, 'Now salvation, and strength, and the kingdom of our God, and the power of His Christ...'" (Rev. 12:10).

> Much as Mary broke her alabaster box and poured its precious contents out to anoint Jesus, we must learn to allow the Holy Spirit to pour out the life of God that is in us.

120

John heard "a loud voice of a great multitude in heaven, saying, 'Alleluia! Salvation and glory and honor and power belong to the Lord our God!'" (Rev. 19:1).

Perhaps we will never fully grasp the wonder of redemption even in eternity. But we can rejoice in it and experience more of the reality of the life of Christ in us as we learn to yield to the Holy Spirit within us. He has come to change us into the image of Christ, causing this "treasure in earthen vessels" to shine forth, "that the excellence of the power may be of God and not of us" (2 Cor. 4:7). That treasure must be poured out of the earthen vessel if it is to profit the kingdom of God. Much as Mary broke her alabaster box and poured its precious contents out to anoint Jesus, we must learn to allow the Holy Spirit to pour out the life of God that is in us.

Cultivating a relationship with the Holy Spirit requires yielding to Him at every point where our wills, our thoughts and our desires differ with His divine purpose for our lives. The Holy Spirit comes to dwell in our spirits, filling us with the life of God. He must express that life, however, through our souls—that is, our mind, emotions and will. God's will must become my will, His thoughts my thoughts and His desires my desires expressed through my volition, my mind and my emotions.

As we saw in the tabernacle of Moses, there was a veil between the holy of holies and the holy place that hid the presence of God from the view of the people. Only the high priest could go behind that veil, and he only once a year, to atone for the sins of the people. Scripture teaches that, as Christians, we are tabernacles of God, temples of the Holy Spirit (1 Cor. 6:19). Unfortunately, many of us have Jesus "locked up" behind a veil in our spirits. He cannot express His life through our souls because we are determined to express our carnal mind, our warped emotions and our rebellious wills.

As an old-fashioned, holiness, Methodist preacher, I treated the life of Christ that way for seventeen years after I was converted. Jesus was locked in my spirit, just as He was hidden from view behind the veil in Moses' tabernacle. I didn't realize that the life of God was locked in my spirit. I shouted joyfully when I understood that the veil of the temple, which had separated man from God's presence, was rent asunder that day at Calvary. I rejoiced because the opening of that veil signified that I personally could go into God's presence. However, I did not realize that the veil of flesh in my soul kept the Spirit of God from filling my temple.

When God sent the Holy Spirit to earth to dwell in our spirits and make us His temples, He planned to rip open that veil of flesh and allow Jesus to fill our entire sanctuary. His intent was to make our minds become His mind, our wills His will, our emotions His emotions. The Holy Spirit would fill each of our temples with His glory. This glory is not an essence to be seen floating in the shape of a cloud, as we have discussed, but is the presence of God manifest in our lives and filling the church.

When we ask the Person of the Holy Spirit to take His abode inside us, we surrender our all to Him. That being the case, we should have a vital relationship with Him on a daily basis. We can evaluate that relationship by our response to questions like these: Can you articulate what

> It is vital that we learn to yield to the life of the Holy Spirit within us if we are to become bearers of God's glory.

122

He has taught you this week? He is our Teacher. Do you know what the offices of the Holy Spirit are? How many of them has He fulfilled in your life this week? Do you know His voice? Do you study in His classroom and ask Him what His purposes are for you?

YIELDING TO
THE HOLY SPIRIT CHANGES US

We tell the Holy Spirit that our lives are His home. When He comes into our lives and finds things foreign to Him, He follows His mandate to clean us, change us and fill us full of the Godhead. He comes to teach us because He knows we are ignorant. He comes to clean us because He knows we are dirty. He comes to give us life because He knows we are dead. Only through this working of the Holy Spirit in our lives will we be changed into the image of our Father. The Holy Spirit makes the Bible come alive, writes it on the tablets of our hearts and changes our natures, replacing Adam's fallen nature with Christ's divine nature.

123

It is vital that we learn to yield to the life of the Holy Spirit within us if we are to become bearers of God's glory. One of the ways we yield to the Holy Spirit is through praise and worship. (See chapter 6.) The Holy Spirit enters the sanctuary of our spirits and sets our lives in harmony with the throne of God through worship.

Another way we yield to the Holy Spirit is by allowing Him to pray through us. There is a clear teaching about prayer coming to the church. Prayer involves more than bringing our want lists to the Father. Many times we don't know what we need. There is Someone else in us who prays according to the will of God for us. As Paul declared:

> Likewise the Spirit also helps in our weaknesses. For we do not know what we should pray for as we ought, but the Spirit Himself makes intercession for us with groanings which cannot be uttered. Now He who searches the hearts knows what the mind of the Spirit is, because He makes intercession for the saints according to the will of God.
> —ROMANS 8:26–27

It is imperative that we learn to experience these divine intercessions if we are to claim the promise of the next verse, "And we know that all things work together for good to those who love God, to those who are the called according to His purpose" (v. 28). The Holy Spirit prays according to what is in the Father's heart, because He was in the covenant before the foundation of the world. Because we don't know what is in the Father's heart, we don't know how to pray as we ought—but the Teacher does. So He comes to teach us to pray according to His will, which is ultimately to make us like Christ.

Paul makes this clear when he continues, "For whom He foreknew, He also predestined to be conformed to the image of His Son, that He might be the firstborn among many brethren" (v. 29). Allowing the Holy Spirit to pray through us is an important part of our being conformed to His image.

Besides yielding to the Holy Spirit in praise and worship and allowing Him to pray through us, we must also allow Him to cleanse us in order that we might be bearers of His glory. It is here where we are tempted to ignore the voice of the Holy Spirit. We do not develop sensitivity to Him, for we resist His convicting power that points to our need for change. We delight in His speaking through us in heavenly languages and bringing gifts and power. But we find it more difficult when He comes as the Scriptures teach us, with a broom, a fan, a fire and fuller's soap. It is then that He is intent on cleansing the temple that has belonged to Adam and still reflects the self-life that has controlled our thoughts, our emotions and our decisions.

> If we take our "I" to the cross, we can exchange it there for the I AM. Then the Holy Spirit moves into every area of our personality, and the veil of flesh begins to fall away.

Though the Holy Spirit speaks in heavenly languages and gives gifts, that is not the reason He came. His mandate is to change our natures and to unveil the nature of Jesus in us. He came to reveal Jesus to us as our Bridegroom and to bring to life the written Word until it becomes the living Christ to us. Then we will show forth His glory, allowing His life to be manifest in every area of our lives.

This is why the apostle Paul could declare that it is "Christ in you, the hope of glory" (Col. 1:27). One day Christ will fill our temples with His glory. No one can make that happen except the Holy Spirit. He came to split the veil of flesh open

125

and let Christ out of our spirits to fill our minds, our wills and our emotions, and to quicken our mortal bodies as well (Rom. 8:11).

It is important to understand that this declaration of "Christ in you" does not deny the reality of the literal Person of Jesus. He is our High Priest who "always lives to make intercession for [us]" (Heb. 7:25). He invited Thomas to feel the scars of His hands and side. Those scars are still there, and that body now appears in the presence of God for us (Heb. 9:24). We are looking for Jesus to appear again, so that our decaying bodies can be changed and fashioned like unto that body of glory (Phil. 3:21). That is the hope of the church.

However, the work of the Holy Spirit is to reveal the glory of Jesus in us. As long as we are in control, He can't be. The "I" nature wants to rule, having my way and exercising my rights, never allowing the Holy Spirit to do what He came to do. If we take our "I" to the cross, we can exchange it there for the I AM. Then the Holy Spirit moves into every area of our personality, and the veil of flesh begins to fall away. We begin to realize that we don't think as we used to think. The truth will dawn on us: "These aren't my thoughts." Then we understand Paul's injunction to "Let this mind be in you which was also in Christ Jesus" (Phil. 2:5). He also admonishes:

> Whatever things are true, whatever things are noble, whatever things are just, whatever things are pure, whatever things are lovely, whatever things are of good report...meditate on these things.
> —PHILIPPIANS 4:8

The Holy Spirit begins to replace Adam's carnal mind with the mind of Christ so we can think as our Daddy thinks. Then He changes our rebellious wills as well. As we keep surrendering to the Holy Spirit, He begins to take the Father's will that we know nothing about and move into our wills. He makes our wills His will and His will our will, if we say yes to Him. As we yield to the Holy Spirit's work within us, we begin to walk with God and to become the will of God.

In the same way, our emotions need to be changed by the Holy Spirit. Some of us may declare, "I am not emotional."

God says, "I know, that is why I have to 'work you over.'" Our emotions constitute one-third of our soul. If we do not express His emotions, that area of our personality is dead. When the Holy Spirit moves into our temples, He comes to get our houses in order—not just for eternity, but so we can show forth His glory now.[1]

127

A SERVANT SPIRIT
REFLECTS THE GLORY

We discussed the "role" of the Holy Spirit to become the Servant when we explained the Covenant made in the Godhead that would result in the Father having a family. After bringing the seed of God to earth and placing that divine life into Mary's womb, the Holy Spirit guided and empowered every aspect of Jesus' life, death and resurrection. He was the One Jesus sent to earth with the divine task of making us a part of the family of God. Though He is God, He works as the servant of God to fulfill the divine purposes of God in our lives.

That is not to say that the Son of God did not become a servant as well. The Scriptures are clear that Jesus "made himself of no reputation, and took upon him the form of a servant, and was made in the likeness of men: And being found in fashion as a man, he humbled himself, and became obedient unto death, even the death of the cross" (Phil 2:7−8, KJV). The spirit of the Servant characterizes the Godhead and therefore is an inherent characteristic of the glory of God—it represents His very nature. In order for us to reflect the glory of God in our lives, we must answer the call to servanthood.

> Becoming a love slave involves coming to the Father and declaring, "I choose to be a love slave."

It is quite possible that our definition of success differs dramatically from God's idea of true greatness. Jesus told His disciples, "Whoever desires to become great among you, let him be your servant. And whoever desires to be first among you, let him be your slave." (Matt. 20:26−27). We must learn to value what God values and esteem what He esteems. Perhaps the truth of servanthood is not an exciting revelation, but without allowing it to become a reality in our lives, we will not become bearers of His glory.

The apostle Paul understood servanthood clearly, declaring, "For though I am free from all men, I have made myself a servant to all, that I might win the more" (1 Cor. 9:19). What Paul actually said was that he made himself a slave to serve everyone in order to bring them to an understanding of

128

the gospel. What was Paul's perspective of servanthood? He was a Hebrew who was well acquainted with the Law. He knew that during the time of the Old Testament, slaves were freed every seventh year. When a slave was freed, he could choose to stay with his master. He would not be a bondslave any longer, but would become a love slave. If he chose to do that, he declared it publicly by laying his head on the doorpost and allowing someone to bore a hole in his ear. By placing an earring in his bored ear, he declared he was no longer a bondslave, but was by choice a love slave for the rest of his life. (See Exodus 21:1–6.)

For a long time I voiced a prayer and didn't really know what I was asking. I prayed, "Father, open my ears, and let me be where I can hear You." As I was studying the Word, I learned that to have your ear "digged" or opened means to have it "bored." The psalmist cried, "My ears You have opened..." (Ps. 40:6).

The opening of our ear to hear God's voice requires the process of having it bored, as was the ear of the love slave. Becoming a love slave involves coming to the Father and declaring, "I am not serving You for promotion or position. I'm not serving You for pay or for profit, vacation or benefits. I'm serving You because I love the family spirit. I choose to be a love slave."

If we have to say that we cannot hear God speak to us, perhaps we are affirming that we are not choosing to be servants. A love slave–*doulos*–is a servant with a bored ear who, without hesitation, reservation or further information does what the Master says. There is nothing in the love slave that wants to refuse. He never expects to choose another profession or

129

seek another master. He serves because of love and because he wants to represent his master.

A servant is not someone who does something with gritted teeth or has left skid marks along the way in following Jesus. He is not someone who does a certain task because he is not qualified to do something greater. Nor is he a person "put down" to a low status because of race, creed or color. A servant is someone who has *chosen* to reflect in his life the family image—the glory—of God.

Servanthood is determined by who we *are,* not by what we *do.* True servanthood involves heart reality. We must learn to value ourselves and every other believer according to our relationship to the Lord Jesus Christ—as children of the same family—rather than by our positions or titles. Every person must be valued for who he is rather than for what he does. What we do should be a result of who we are. When we begin to see ourselves as servants of God, it won't make any difference to us what we are asked to do. If we are to reflect the glory of God, we must develop a servant's heart. We must learn to humble ourselves as Jesus did, emptying Himself of all privilege and every title. He chose to become the obedient Servant to carry out His Father's wishes. Because of His great humbling, the Father has highly honored Him (Phil. 2:7–11).

As a servant, the Scriptures teach that we will be "in honor giving preference to one another" (Rom. 12:10). Jesus preferred us above Himself, willingly suffering the supreme sacrifice of giving His life to redeem us. On the eve of His death, during the Last Supper with His disciples, He gave us one more glimpse of the family spirit. Knowing that the Father had given all things into His hands, Jesus took a towel and girded Himself and washed His disciples' feet. (See John 13:4–5.) After His resurrection from the dead, having won the supreme victory over sin, Jesus still revealed the humble servant spirit to His disciples on the morning when He cooked their breakfast on the shore of the lake. "As soon as they had come to land, they saw a fire of coals there, and fish laid on it, and bread. Jesus said to them…Come and eat breakfast" (John 21:9–10, 12).

Responding to the call to servanthood involves scrutinizing the attitudes and motivations that form the basis of our character. Solomon taught that "as [a man] thinks in his heart, so is he" (Prov. 23:7). If in our hearts we see ourselves as wonderful people with tremendous potential for becoming great in some sphere of life or ministry, we have not yet responded to the call to servanthood. We are not yet acting like a servant. When we see ourselves as blood-bought children of God, no longer belonging to ourselves, our response will be, "Lord, I love You enough to serve You." A true servant heart pursues holiness and purity of motive in service. Our motivation for serving is as important as our service, for God is looking for servant hearts to reflect the spirit of the Lamb. As we allow the Holy Spirit to teach us to become part of the family of God,

> As we allow the Holy Spirit to teach us to become part of the family of God, He will change our motivation and our attitudes to reflect the glory of God.

131

He will change our motivation and our attitudes to reflect the glory of God.

I want to be able to sing like an elder, gray-headed professor who taught me in Bible college. He came into our Pentateuch class and, without any formality of opening remarks, bowed his head, shook his gray hair and began to sing:

> He loves me. He loves me,
> This I know;
> He gave Himself to die for me
> Because He loves me so.

We students ended up on the cement floor crying our eyes out because of the presence of God that filled that classroom. This man was the most brilliant professor of the college—and the most humble. On work days, he was present. When there were leaves to be raked, he was there. Supervisors would say to him, in deference to his age, "Dr. Burkholder, you don't need to do that."

He would say, "Oh, but I do. I am doing it for Jesus." Very often he was heard singing his favorite song, "He loves me. He loves me."

Joy is the desired attitude of a servant. "The joy of the LORD is your strength" (Neh. 8:10). According to Dr. David Schoch, that verse literally reads, "The joy we give God in serving Him gives us back His strength."[2] God's genuine approval of our service becomes strength for us to serve. A servant does each task joyfully. It is written of Jesus, the Servant of all, "Who for the joy that was set before Him endured the cross..." (Heb. 12:2). Jesus' suffering did not destroy His joy. A servant can endure great difficulty because he is convinced that his greatest privilege on earth is to serve God.

Faithfulness further characterizes the servant heart. A servant is a faithful steward or overseer. A *steward* takes care of something that belongs to another person until that one can return to take care of it. As an overseer, he does not require the master to write out all the instructions, but is able to take responsibility within a certain latitude. We are responsible to allow the character of Christ to be developed in us as we yield to the Holy Spirit's conviction and promptings, showing us where we need to be changed.

We will not be rewarded for our educational degrees or our personal excellence, but for our faithful obedience as servants. Our greatest commendation will be for God to say to us, "Well done, thou good and faithful servant" (Matt. 25:21, KJV). He does not commend the *preacher, apostle* or *minister,* but the *servant.* Faithfulness results in our becoming addicted to service.

In the New Testament we read of the inhabitants of the house of Stephanas, who had addicted themselves to ministry (1 Cor. 16:15). The Greek reads, "They made up their minds to serve as servants; they were addicted." Being addicted to something makes you feel as if you can't live without it. The Holy Spirit can cause us to become addicted to servanthood so that we can reflect the glory of God in our lives.

If joy is our attitude, and faithfulness our measure of love, we can describe *humility* as the demeanor of our servant heart. A proud spirit will rarely be joyful, nor will it be faithful to any task that does not satisfy its ego. The spirit of our Father's family is not a spirit of exaltation or pride, but is

133

exemplified in the spirit of the Lamb who sacrificed Himself to redeem us. Humility characterizes those who are full of the Holy Spirit. The spirit of the family of God is the spirit of the prodigal son who has come to himself, is broken and is anxious to come home to Daddy, saying, "Make me like one of your hired servants" (Luke 15:19).

FOOTWASHING IS REQUIRED OF A SERVANT

We cannot respond to the call to servanthood without being secure in our identity as a person. Without knowing who we are in God, we will never choose to become servants. The greater the understanding we have of who we are, the less we feel we have to "prove" to ourselves and others. Jesus is our example again of the ultimate servant, one whom we must emulate. On the night of the Last Supper with His disciples, the Scripture says:

> Jesus, knowing that the Father had given all things into His hands, and that He had come from God and was going to God, rose from supper and laid aside His garments, took a towel and girded Himself. After that, He poured water into a basin and bean to wash the disciples' feet, and to wipe them with the towel with which He was girded.
> —John 13:3–5

Jesus knew who He was. He knew that everything in the world belonged to Him. With that knowledge, He rose from

134

supper, took a towel, poured water into a basin and began to wash the disciples' feet.[3]

When Peter remonstrated at this act, the Lord declared a very strong warning that we must consider. He said to Peter, "If I do not wash you, you have no part with Me" (v. 8). What does He mean, "no part with Me"? The disciples had left all to follow Jesus, even with so little understanding of who He was and what was His true mission.

This washing of the disciples' feet was no kind gesture or simple picture of the Lord's humbling Himself once more. According to Jesus, it was necessary in order for them to have relationship with Him. It signified the neutralizing of the "earth touch"—the contact with the earth that lies under the curse, which God can never accept. It is completely contrary to God's mind. Though we must live here in an ungodly world, we must develop a great sensitivity to the dust, the contamination of earth's atmosphere. Without allowing ourselves to be cleansed from the dirt that clings to us through our involuntary contact with the world, we can have no part in the life of God that requires purity and holiness.

Consider the perfect Son of God walking amidst the sinfulness of mankind. How He must have suffered in His spirit and soul from its evil contrast to His holiness. Many people, including some Christians, can tolerate a lot of "dirt" without being bothered by it. They are not sensitive to the sinful atmosphere that surrounds them; therefore, they do not feel their need to be washed and cleansed from its contamination. We must develop this sensitivity to the touch of death that clings to us through association with the world.

This sensitivity will be seen in many ways in our Christian

walk. We will react violently to our own conversation if it does not reflect the Spirit of Christ. As cleansed Christians, we will closely scrutinize what we read, for we do not wish to contaminate our thoughts with the philosophies and unclean spirit of the world. We will cultivate a sensitivity that will cause us pain when there is anything touching us, influencing our lives, that does not agree with the Word of the Lord for our lives.

> We will not be rewarded for our educational degrees or our personal excellence, but for our faithful obedience as servants.

The symbolic act of footwashing holds great significance, for it reveals the glory of God in our lives. Jesus taught that we ought to wash one another's feet. There is a place for humbling ourselves literally to wash the feet of a fellow Christian. But the significance of that act is the spiritual washing it brings, allowing the love of Christ to flow between two believers. It is the spirit of meekness that helps one who has become touched, tainted or overtaken in a fault in their Christian lives.

The apostle Paul declared:

> Brethren, if a man is overtaken in any trespass, you who are spiritual restore such a one in a spirit of gentleness, considering yourself lest you also be tempted.
>
> —GALATIANS 6:1

Walking along in our life in God, we may be overtaken and our feet may be caught in a place of corruption and sin. Instead of judging or condemning each other, we are taught to humble ourselves and, in a spirit of meekness, restore our brother or sister, knowing that tomorrow it may be us that needs to be restored.

It is unfortunate that even in the church, too often when we see a brother or sister with dirt on his or her feet, instead of washing them, we throw more dirt. We are more ready to criticize them for their faults than to help them get rid of the faults. The washing of feet signifies symbolically that we must make it our business to humble ourselves, knowing our own frailty, weakness and lowliness of mind, and help them to remove the fault or sin that is contaminating their walk with the Lord.

Such an attitude of humility will reveal the glory of God—His character—in humility as it was revealed on that night when Jesus took the towel and washed His disciples' feet. The power of God will be there to enable us to have a greater part with Jesus than we had before the humbling and washing—in our own lives and in the lives of others.

If the church is to walk in purity, we will have to learn the path of footwashing as Jesus taught it. We will have to learn to live with the body of Christ as Paul taught us to do, "speaking the truth in love" (Eph. 4:15). We will begin to care as much for each other as we do for ourselves. Much more could be said about walking in humility, meekness and love for the brethren. But as we take the first step toward these integral characteristics of Christ, we will learn firsthand how the glory of God will be revealed to us and through us in our obedience.

The glory that is to be revealed through the church, and

specifically through our clay temples, will be a result of our complete obedience to these commands of Christ. There is coming such a wonderful hour of glorious revelation of God to the church—one that we cannot imagine or begin to describe. We can only turn to the Scriptures that declare it and allow the Holy Spirit to fill our hearts with expectation and hope, and a deep desire to complete our obedience to Him so that we can be a part of the glory to be revealed.

Chapter 9

Glory
in the Church

A Mature Body of Christ

All of the apostle Paul's epistles and most of the New Testament, apart from the Gospels, are letters written to the early church. They declare plainly that the purposes of God are culminated in the final establishment of a glorious church that is characterized by *holiness, unity* and *power*. Every believer is supposed to be planted in a local church where he or she can function in his or her God-given abilities to supply what the body of Christ needs. (See Ephesians 4:16.) God intends to manifest His glory ultimately in and through His church, which is His body in the earth.

> . . . Christ also loved the church, and gave himself for it; that he might sanctify and cleanse it with the washing of water by the word, that he might present it to himself a glorious church, not having

spot, or wrinkle, or any such thing; but that it should be holy and without blemish.

—EPHESIANS 5:25−27, KJV

We have discussed how the glory of God is developed in individual believers' lives to show forth His *moral character* and *nature*. And of course, it is individual believers who comprise the church. There is an aspect of the glory of God that involves a *manifestation of His visible presence* that is peculiar to the church corporately. Perhaps we could use the analogy of a diamond that reflects and refracts rays of light. If each ray of light were a believer, the entire diamond would be the church with its many facets capable of reflecting the glorious light of God collectively.

> As the character of God is released through the lives of believers corporately, He will have a glorious church without spot or wrinkle.

140

The apostle Peter declared of the church:

But ye are a chosen generation, a royal priesthood, an holy nation, a peculiar people; that ye should shew forth the praises of him who hath called you out of darkness into his marvellous light: Which in time past were not a people, but are now the people of God: which had not

obtained mercy, but now have obtained mercy.
—1 PETER 2:9–10, KJV

God's glory must be manifested in the *personal holiness* of each believer. It is multiplied synergistically when those believers form the corporate expression of Christ in the church. God's glory must be revealed in the *power of each believer's transformed life.* It displays His redemptive power most effectively through the corporate body. And God's glory must result in *unity,* reconciling the believer to His God, to himself and to his neighbor. The result of that reconciliation reveals the glory of God through the unity of His body, the church. As we look at these three aspects of the glory of God revealed through His church—holiness, power and unity—we can glimpse the reality of the visible presence of the glorious church that God is preparing in the earth.

141

HOLINESS IN THE CHURCH

In the context of the church, as individual temples of clay release the treasure that is within them, God's glory is going to fill the earth. We need to understand the significance of being a part of the church in the earth, rather than just "going to church" on Sunday. There is a much greater responsibility for every believer to be a functioning part of the body of Christ in the earth than we have realized.

As the character of God is released through the lives of believers corporately, He will have a glorious church without spot or wrinkle. We are going home in His holiness. When Lucifer fell from heaven, God also kicked out rebellion, selfishness and independence. He is not going to allow it to enter again. Holiness is not an option—it is a command. And holiness will characterize the church of Jesus Christ. In order to walk in holiness with the body of Christ, we need to be cleansed continually from the power of sin and the uncleanness it works in us.

The Bible declares:

> But if we walk in the light as He is in the light, we have fellowship with one another, and the blood of Jesus Christ His Son cleanses us from all sin.
> —1 JOHN 1:7

We never outgrow the need for the blood of Jesus to cleanse us so that we can be reconciled to our brothers and sisters in the body of Christ. If we understand the priority of God's heart to reveal His glory through His church, we will take the responsibility to walk carefully with our brothers and sisters so we will not hinder the purposes of God.

The Lord has showed me five specific things from which the church must be delivered in order to reflect the holiness of God and show forth His glory. These are *denominationalism, tradition, prejudice, custom* and *culture*. It may help to briefly summarize each of these ills that plague the church and hinder her from showing forth the glory of God.

DENOMINATIONALISM

Denominationalism occurs when denominational doctrines are taught with dogmatic finality so that greater streams of truth that would flow through the church are limited. It is characterized by elitism, legalism and judgmental attitudes that separate believers from each other and obscure the true church that Christ is building.

HUMAN TRADITION

Human tradition is defined by the dictionary as "an inherited, established or customary pattern of thought, action or behavior; the handing down of information, beliefs and customs by word of mouth or by example from one generation to another without written instruction." Because man's carnal mind has interpreted many of the Scriptures being used in the church today, the Holy Spirit, the divine Teacher who wrote the Book, has not been allowed to reveal truth to our spirits. As a result we have developed religious practices that are "comfort zones" to our church mentality. Failing to "rightly [divide] the word of truth" (2 Tim. 2:15), instead we have read it according to the instruction of men. I believe God is creating in the hearts of believers a new hunger and thirst for his Word. As the Holy Spirit reveals His Word to our hearts, the church will be cleansed from traditions of men and be filled with the life-giving waters of the Holy Spirit.

143

PREJUDICE

Prejudice, which results from unreasonable biases, judgments or opinions held in disregard of facts, breeds suspicion, intolerance or hatred and has no place in Christ's church. Whether it is against race, gender, sect, class or status, prejudice will keep us from receiving the truth of God as revealed by the Holy Spirit, and it will hinder us from showing forth the glory of God in the church.

CULTURE

Culture is the concepts, habits, arts, institutions and refinements of thought, manners, and taste that characterize our native environment and seem "right" to us. For that reason, some missionaries have exported more culture than Christ life, attempting to conform others to their own lifestyle. We have to be delivered from our bondage to culture in order to allow Christ to move in us and through us to any culture.

> As the Holy Spirit reveals His Word to our hearts, the church will be cleansed from traditions of men and be filled with the life-giving waters of the Holy Spirit.

144

CUSTOM

A *custom* is defined as "a long-established practice considered as unwritten law; a uniform practice by common consent of a society to such an extent that it has taken on the force of the law." The apostle Paul's letter to the Galatian church denounces the Jews who were trying to add their customs as requirements for salvation. The same thing can happen today. We can get caught up in some legalistic custom we believe is necessary to our salvation. Entire religious systems have been developed around external rituals that in effect deny the sacrifice of Jesus. Unless we place our trust in the death and resurrection of Christ for our salvation, and that of the world, we have no hope of being saved.

The Holy Spirit is faithful to speak truth to us as we open our hearts to hear Him. He was sent to guide us into all truth (John 16:13). We need not fear or despair that we will not know how to be delivered from our wrong thinking. As we listen to the Holy Spirit and allow Him to convict and cleanse us, we will be a part of the wonderful revival that is coming to the church.

UNITY IN THE CHURCH

Though we listed power as a second characteristic of the glorious church, I believe the power of God in the church will be manifested as a result of the unity of believers. The Scriptures teach clearly about the power that is released through unity. The psalmist declared:

145

> Behold, how good and how pleasant it is
> For brethren to dwell together in unity!
> It is like the precious oil upon the head,
> Running down the beard,
> The beard of Aaron,
> Running down on the edge of his garments.
> It is like the dew of Hermon,
> Descending upon the mountains of Zion;
> For there the LORD commanded the blessing—
> Life forevermore.
>
> —PSALM 133:1–3, KJV

When Jesus prayed His high priestly prayer, He asked the

Father for unity for His disciples and for all who would believe on their Word—which includes all believers. These are His words:

> That they all may be one; as thou, Father, art in me, and I in thee, that they also may be one in us: that the world may believe that thou hast sent me. And the glory which thou gavest me I have given them; that they may be one, even as we are one: I in them, and thou in me, that they may be made perfect in one; and that the world may know that thou hast sent me, and hast loved them, as thou hast loved me.
> —JOHN 17:21–23, KJV

The Scriptures record this divine prayer for us, giving us hope that certainly the prayers of Jesus will be answered and His request granted. I believe that in a way we have not yet experienced in the church, the power of the unity of believers is going to reveal the glory of God to the world so that they will believe that Jesus is the Savior. *Unity* is a heart issue that centers around fellowship and spiritual realities we all hold in common. It is not *uniformity*. I believe the expressions of the body of Christ can be as varied and colorful as a flower garden and still reflect the glory of God in the earth as a visible representation of His moral character and beauty.

Unity is the state of being made one. According to the dictionary, it means to have "a oneness of mind, or feeling, as when people live in concord, harmony or agreement." Unity does not preclude diversity, as the Scriptures are careful to explain. Metaphors and allegories in the Bible that describe

the redeemed people of God depict a community characterized by unity with diversity and diversity in unity. For example,
the Bible describes diversities of manifestations and gifts, but
one Spirit (1 Cor. 12:4).

The apostle Paul illustrates the divine purpose for the unity
and diversity of Christ's body by referring to the human body.
He explains that the human body has many members with different functions, all necessary to the health of the body. He
then exhorts, however, that while the gifts and ministries in
the church vary, they must not be allowed to cause division by
drawing attention to the gifted person or creating cliques
within the church.

Paul insists that the redeemed community is one organic
whole consisting of diverse members. That diversity is intended
to bring a divine variety of ministry to the whole body of Christ
for the common good of all. A beautiful picture emerges when
we envision a body of people, all variously gifted by the Holy
Spirit, ministering in love to one another. As the church leaves
the immaturity of competition and manifests maturity of unity
in Christian compassion, she will show forth the glory of God
to the whole world.

The body of Christ cannot endure competition between its
members. We need each other if we are going to fulfill God's
divine purpose in this earth. When we fail to flow with every
other member of the body, we are rebelling against God's purpose for His corporate body and are defeating our own personal destiny. We are injuring other members in the body and
withholding the beautiful, corporate Christ that God desires
to manifest to the world.

Here is the supreme glory of the Christian man: He is part

147

of the body of Christ on earth. I believe with all my heart that the church is going to display a greater unity than we have seen through all of history. The Holy Spirit is going to reveal Jesus Christ to the world through the church: "To Him be glory in the church" (Eph. 3:21).[1]

POWER IN THE
CHURCH THROUGH UNITY

Unity can be dangerous. When the Golden Gate Bridge in California was restored a few years ago, the media published a warning to the one million people who planned to walk across it the first night it was open. They warned them that if they walked together in rank—in a unified pattern—the bridge would fall from the impact. Marching bands often break cadence when they cross a bridge. That is a natural example of the power that spiritual unity can bring when the church walks together as one.

> As we mature in Christ we will become seekers of unity rather than seekers of our own gain.

When Jesus declared that through unity the world would know that the Father sent Him (John 17:21), He gave us one of the greatest keys to power in evangelism. It is clear that there is a power in unity that will draw the world to Jesus. Unity attracts people. Everyone wants to be on a united team. The world knows that unity is impossible for people who are bent on making a name for themselves. We need only look at the

148

current problems among high-paid, superstar athletes to recognize this fact. The world will recognize the difference unity makes to the chaos of personal ambition and one-upmanship. Living in unity brings a refreshing, revitalizing force to our lives, in part simply because we have been relieved of the tension created by competing with others.

Maturity is required for the church to seek to dwell in unity as the Scriptures command. When the apostle Paul exhorted the Ephesian church to unity in spirit and in faith, he admonished them:

> That we should no longer be children, tossed to
> and fro...but, speaking the truth in love, may grow
> up in all things into Him who is the head—Christ.
> —EPHESIANS 4:14–15

As we mature in Christ we will become seekers of unity rather than seekers of our own gain. The time is past for believers to seek their own ministries and build their own reputations at the expense of others.

I wonder if we realize the time and energy consumed by churches as they work to put out "brush fires" caused by carnal competitions? The effort could be put to better use by igniting the flames of the Holy Spirit, which would enlighten this darkened world. The enemy energizes our petty differences. He knows the power of unity in the church and fears it exceedingly. We must seek the maturity that will result in unity in the church and release the power of God as we have never known it.

The apostle Paul quoted the prophet who declared, "Eye hath not seen, nor ear heard, neither have entered into the

149

heart of man, the things which God hath prepared for them that love him" (1 Cor. 2:9, KJV). He was referring in context to the spirit of revelation that we receive from God, not from the world. There is much revelation that awaits us as sons of God who are walking in the fullness of the Spirit.

TRANSFIGURED GLORY IN THE CHURCH

As we discussed the pattern of the Son as He walked on earth, filled with the Holy Spirit, we understood that the Holy Spirit was with Jesus from birth, to His baptism, His temptation, His ministry, in His transfiguration, death and resurrection. And we understand that the Holy Spirit will empower our lives in the same way He did the life of Jesus to live victoriously and conquer sin, self and the devil.

I believe God intends for believers to follow the pattern Son while on earth. We do this by:

- Receiving the life of Christ by being born again

- Being water baptized

- Experiencing the baptism of the Holy Spirit

- Being led into the wilderness, as Jesus was, to overcome the enemy of our souls, defeating him as Jesus did when He declared, "It is written" (Matt. 4:4)

Our wildernesses may take many forms—having to leave our relatives, friends, doctrinal positions, ambitions or plans to follow Christ. We can all testify to a place of temptation where we have had to establish our determination to worship God alone.

But how many of us have thought of the next step in Jesus' life, that which took Him to the Mount of Transfiguration? It was there that He experienced the supernatural unveiling of the glory of God and heard the voice from heaven that once again affirmed, "This is My beloved Son, in whom I am well pleased" (Matt. 17:5). Does a similar experience not occur in the lives of believers?

We understand that we will be required to go to the cross and be crucified with Christ in order to enjoy resurrection power in our lives. Thus, of the seven steps of redemption, all but the fifth one—being transfigured—seem easy to apply to the life of the church. As I was meditating on the Scriptures, the Holy Spirit showed me that what was revealed in the transfiguration of Jesus was Adam as he would have become if he had not fallen. He would have become a mature son of God who pleased the Father in all he did.

> Abandoned surrender to God individually and corporately as the body of Christ is the key to being transfigured, so the glory of God will be seen in us and shine forth through us.

151

The Scriptures refer to Christ as the last Adam (1 Cor. 15:45). As Christ grew in favor with God and man and did His

Father's will, He became the mature Son whom the Father could affirm. It was then that He entered into the ministry God had ordained for Him, directed by the Holy Spirit. Everything He did on earth was by the power of the Holy Spirit working through His humanity.

As I continued meditating on the wonder of the transfiguration, the Holy Spirit directed me to the Book of Romans. He asked me what the word *transformed* meant in Romans 12:2. As I studied the word, I understood that it could be translated as "transfigured." It comes from the word *metamorphosis,* and means to be changed or metamorphosed.

I trembled at the truth God was making clear to my heart. The apostle Paul instructs us:

> I beseech you therefore, brethren, by the mercies of God, that you present your bodies a living sacrifice, holy, acceptable to God, which is your reasonable service...be transformed by the renewing of your mind.
>
> —ROMANS 12:1–2

What Paul is really saying is for us to be transfigured by the power of the Holy Spirit living within us.

Abandoned surrender to God individually and corporately as the body of Christ is the key to being transfigured, so the glory of God will be seen in us and shine forth through us. His Word, the Living Word, working in us His good pleasure will transform us so that the power of God will be released through us. Then we will go forth, as Jesus did after His transfiguration, and work the works of God that He has ordained for us to do.

THE "GREATER WORKS" CHURCH

Jesus declared to His disciples:

> Verily, verily, I say unto you, He that believeth on me, the works that I do shall he do also; and greater works than these shall he do; because I go unto my Father. And whatsoever ye shall ask in my name, that will I do, that the Father may be glorified in the Son. If ye shall ask any thing in my name, I will do it.
>
> —JOHN 14:12–14, KJV

There has been much speculation as to what "greater works" really means for the body of Christ. Some have suggested that the healing and miracles Jesus did would be done through the church, but in greater numbers than Jesus was able to do by being one man limited to one place at a time. Others refer to the greater revelation of the truths of God such as Paul received and recorded for us in the christological epistles. Whatever our idea of greater works, we want to be a part of the supernatural work of God in the earth that shows forth His glory as He intended us to do.

Jesus raised Lazarus from the dead after he was buried for four days. The natural evaluation of his condition was that he "stinketh" (John 11:39, KJV). There is much death in the church today, much burial of that which is stinking. Many times we have yearned in our hearts, as Martha and Mary did, crying, "If You had been here, my brother would not have died" (v. 32). We lament, "Lord, if You had brought revival sooner, our brothers would not have died." We grieve over our family members and church members who are cold or lukewarm, and weep over the disunity within and among churches in our communities.

The Lord has promised restoration, raising up a mighty army in the earth. You ask, *How can that be possible? How can we expect to see such a resurrection?* Those questions reveal that we have not yet understood the magnitude of the coming revival—of the "greater works" church. The prophet declared, "For the earth will be filled with the knowledge of the glory of the LORD, as the waters cover the sea" (Hab. 2:14, NAS).

> We are part of the present fulfillment of His promise to have a glorious church without spot or wrinkle. It is God's appointed time to favor His people.

As members of God's church in the earth today, we are part of the present fulfillment of His promise to have a glorious church without spot or wrinkle. We should echo the prayer of the psalmist: "Thou wilt arise and have compassion on Zion; for it is time to be gracious to her, for the appointed time has come" (Ps. 102:13, NAS). *Zion,* in Scripture, represents the church, the people of God, through whom God desires to manifest His glory. It is God's appointed time to favor His people.

As the glory of God begins to be manifested through the church, it won't happen just in local congregations. It will

154

flow into homes, communities and business places. As it increases, it won't be just droplets of life-giving rain here and there. It will be a flood running to those "in deserts and mountains, in dens and caves of the earth" (Heb. 11:38).

Our government, our church denominations, our social organizations, our school systems, our industries—many of which have become corrupt, motivated by self-promotion, serving for gold and silver and ruled by covetous practices—will all be changed by the power of God's divine presence. This revival will be so powerful that throughout our land we will see a return to the great historical foundations of this nation, which declares that in God we trust.

As we believers behold Christ in His glory, we will realize that He has not withheld resurrection life from us. It is sin that has prevented it—unbelief, carnal competition, covetousness and so forth. As we respond to the Word of God that is saying, "Do not be conformed to this world, but be transformed by the renewing of your mind" (Rom. 12:2), we will hear a sweet sound of heaven as the gates are raised and the flood waters of revival are released.

Holiness will result in *unity* that will release the supernatural *power* of God as we have never known it through the church. We are living in the greatest hour the church has ever known. Already we are experiencing wonderful outpourings of revival in many parts of the earth.

The world will see the glory of God in His body, just as the disciples beheld the glory of God on the Mount of Transfiguration. As the revelation of the Living Word becomes manifest in each of our lives, we will become the glorious church God intended us to be. My prayer for the church

155

today is powerfully expressed in the apostle Paul's prayer for all the "faithful in Christ Jesus" (Eph. 1:1):

> That the God of our Lord Jesus Christ, the Father of glory, may give unto you the spirit of wisdom and revelation in the knowledge of him: The eyes of your understanding being enlightened; that ye may know what is the hope of his calling, and what the riches of the glory of his inheritance in the saints, and what is the exceeding greatness of his power to us-ward who believe, according to the working of his mighty power, which he wrought in Christ, when he raised him from the dead, and set him at his own right hand in the heavenly places, far above all principality, and power, and might, and dominion, and every name that is named, not only in this world, but also in that which is to come.
>
> —EPHESIANS 1:17–21, KJV

As the church grows to maturity, this divine life of Christ, the revelation of who He is in all His glory, will be seen by the world through believers. Our unity with God will result in our unity with one another. As we allow the Holy Spirit to divide asunder our souls and spirits, Christ's love will be manifested toward one another and to a lost world. (See Hebrews 4:12.) Not only will our lives be transformed, but also we will rejoice to see a great harvest of souls in answer to Jesus' prayer to the Father, "that the world may believe that You sent me" (John 17:21).

When Jesus brings many sons to glory—sons with knowledge, those who cry "Abba, Father," and who are living by divine revelation—the prophet's declaration concerning Him will be fulfilled: "He shall see the labor of His soul, and be satisfied" (Isa. 53:11).

Chapter 10

Glory to Be Revealed

God's Dream Realized—Forever!

I f we have found it a challenging task to articulate the eternal realities of the glory of God as they are revealed to us in His Word, it would seem presumptuous to think we could adequately describe the glory of God that is yet to be revealed in fulfillment of His Word. Yet, our eternal hope lies in the ultimate establishing of God's kingdom, not only in our hearts, but in every "place" that exists in our eternity future. We can encourage each other with the scriptures that establish our hope for eternal bliss in the wonderful presence of God's glory, though their deepest meaning may not have been completely revealed to us yet.

The New Testament writers were motivated by this hope of eternal glory. Their lives were focused on making sure they were a part of the kingdom of God in such a way that they could experience that glory and could influence as many as possible to be a part of it. The apostle Paul wrote to the Colossians of this hope:

> We give thanks to the God and Father of our Lord
> Jesus Christ, praying always for you, since we
> heard of your faith in Christ Jesus and of your love
> for all the saints; because of the hope which is laid
> up for you in heaven, of which you heard before in
> the word of the truth of the gospel...
>
> —Colossians 1:3–5

And Titus characterized this hope as the goal for our living holy lives:

> For the grace of God that brings salvation has
> appeared to all men, teaching us that, denying
> ungodliness and worldly lusts, we should live
> soberly, righteously, and godly in the present age,
> looking for the blessed hope and glorious appearing
> of our great God and Savior Jesus Christ, who gave
> Himself for us, that He might redeem us from every
> lawless deed and purify for Himself His own special
> people, zealous for good works.
>
> —Titus 2:11–14, NKJV

In our inadequate attempt to trace the glory of God through the Scriptures, we have defined the glory of God in summary as *God's moral beauty and perfection of character; God's moral beauty as a visible presence; and praise and honor that God's creatures give to Him.* As the Scriptures reveal to us the holy character and loving nature of God and His desire to have intimate relationship with mankind, we are moved to bow our hearts and worship Him, giving Him the praise and honor He deserves. In that place of worship, redemption takes place in our hearts, leading us to greater revelation of His glory, which in turn deepens our worship. This intimacy of relationship will cause us to continually become bearers of His glory in greater dimensions.

We glimpsed His divine glory in the Godhead, before the beginning of time, as They sacrificed for each other to fulfill Their dream for a family. The Word of God consented to becoming the Son of God, suffering the *kenosis*, all that the "emptying" of His deity would require for His incarnation, death, burial and resurrection (Phil. 2). John declares in his Gospel, "And the Word became flesh, and dwelt among us, and we beheld His glory, glory as of the only begotten from the Father, full of grace and truth" (John 1:14, NAS). Though the Son of God was wholly God, the Scriptures teach us that He lived in dependence on the Holy Spirit as the Son of Man, showing forth the glory of the Father to the world.

161

The Holy Spirit became the Servant to bring the Word to earth, to empower Him in His life, ministry, death, resurrection and ascension as the divine Son of God. The Holy Spirit remains the Servant on earth to do the same for us, depositing the divine seed of God into our spirits when we are born again and empowering us to experience the divine reality of "Christ in you, the hope of glory" (Col. 1:27). Jesus said to His disciples, "And I will ask the Father, and He will give you another Helper, that He may be with you forever" (John 14:16, NAS).

We witnessed the Father's hurt-love as revealed to us through the types and shadows of the Old Testament, leading

His sacrificial Lamb to slaughter as a means of atonement for sin. Even after Jesus had walked with His disciples on earth, they could not grasp the love of the Father. We can hear the pain in Jesus' heart when He responds to their request to see the Father:

> Philip saith unto him, Lord, shew us the Father, and it sufficeth us. Jesus saith unto him, Have I been so long time with you, and yet hast thou not known me, Philip? He that hath seen me hath seen the Father; and how sayest thou then, Shew us the Father?
>
> —JOHN 14:8–9, KJV

The Scriptures clearly reveal to us how each Person of the Trinity of God has poured out Their divine love on mankind to redeem us from sin so that God could have the family He has desired.

162

We visited the blissful scenes in the Garden of Eden with the parents of our race, Adam and Eve, who were clothed with the glory of God in their innocence, living in unbroken communion and fellowship with their Creator. The terrible consequences of their tragic choice to live independently from God, disobeying His command not to eat of the tree of the knowledge of good and evil required the sacrifice of Christ, the second Adam, at Calvary. If Adam and Eve had chosen to obey God, the character of God would have been formed in them through their obedience as they matured in relationship with Him. Now, as we receive the sacrifice of Christ and allow His blood to save us from our sins, we can bring our sinful nature to His cross and exchange it for the nature and character of God as we choose to obey Him and mature in our relationship with Him.

It would be easy to blame Lucifer, the serpent in the garden, for the terrible tragedy of the fall of mankind. But it was a choice that Adam and his wife made that created the chaos and death with which we have had to contend through the history of mankind. We beheld the beauty of Lucifer in heaven, in the very presence of the glory of God. The splendor of this created being, his high position of influence around the throne of God is difficult for us to comprehend. Yet perhaps more difficult to grasp, even for theologians, is the *cause* for his high treason against God, on which the scriptures seem to be silent. We dare not speculate, though we can guard our hearts against the "I will ascend" attitude of Lucifer that resulted in his downfall.

> This intimacy of relationship will cause us to continually become bearers of His glory in greater dimensions.

163

Sam Hinn, in a sermon titled "Created to Worship," discusses the role of Lucifer, whose name means "lightbearer," in the worship of heaven. Lucifer's angelic being was filled with precious gems, and it seems as if beautiful musical sounds of worship were a part of his being. He was a cherub who covered in the midst of the throne of God, where the pure worship and glory of God was most intense, where light and sound were most beautiful.

Sam Hinn shares that science has determined that sound and light are closely related in the world of physics. They have discovered that tones on the musical scale each emanate a different color that is not visible to our human sight because of its limitations. They are able to measure sound waves and light waves and actually record the specific color that each sound produces. If God were to re-adjust our human visibility to the light spectrum, we would be able to see these colors as musical notes were played. Imagine what worship would be like as each instrument and each voice are lifted up in worship and praise to God—what a *light show!* The highest purpose of music is to be a vehicle, for God to express His greatness, glory and love to man.

If science is discovering such beautiful relationships between light and sound on earth, we can only imagine what worship can become for believers who are true "light-bearers" of the glory of God. Jesus came to redeem everything the devil stole from us and to reveal His glory to us and through us as we worship the Lamb of God. Our spirits can be clothed once again with the glory of God as Adam and Eve were in the garden. We can enjoy the unbroken communion with God that they did and hear His voice teaching us how to live. As we learn to live lives of worship, we will be empowered with the nature and character of God that Jesus died to make possible. All of this divine glory is ours to experience now, as we determine to live in fellowship with God. Yet the Scriptures indicate there is more to come—more of the glory of God still to be revealed to His "family."

John the Revelator had glimpses of worship around the throne of God that are so unearthly we can hardly relate to them. He describes one scene of worship when "the twenty-four elders fall down before Him who sits on the throne and worship Him who lives forever and ever, and cast their crowns before the throne, saying: 'You are worthy, O Lord, to receive glory and honor and power: for You created all things, and by Your will they exist and were created'" (Rev. 4:10–11). He saw multitudes and even nations worshiping the Lamb around the throne of God. Such exaltation and awesome response can scarcely be imagined in the smallness of our psyches and emotional awareness.

> We need to allow the Holy Spirit to thrill our hearts with a vision of this glory that is to come.

Yet our hearts beat with a yearning to experience the presence of God that we are witnessing around the throne.

Perhaps the most tender picture in Scripture of the glory of God that is to be revealed is that of the bride making herself ready for her bridegroom. We visited the historical type of this bride of Christ in the life of Rebekah, sent for by the servant to become a bride for his master's son Isaac. The choice was hers, to leave all and follow the servant, finally losing sight even of the master's gifts as her eyes glimpsed her beloved, her bridegroom, awaiting her after her long, arduous journey through the wilderness. It is not difficult to relate to this tender love story as we journey through the wilderness of life to reach our Bridegroom. Though the Servant, the Holy Spirit, gives us many gifts that come from the Father, our hearts long to see the face of our Beloved

165

and to know the consummation of our love in Him alone.

Yet the wonder of the description of our Beloved at the marriage supper of the Lamb, as recorded by John the Revelator, can scarcely be grasped by our human imagination:

> And he saith unto me, Write, Blessed are they which are called unto the marriage supper of the Lamb. And he saith unto me, These are the true sayings of God...And I saw heaven opened, and behold a white horse; and he that sat upon him was called Faithful and True, and in righteousness he doth judge and make war. His eyes were as a flame of fire, and on his head were many crowns; and he had a name written, that no man knew, but he himself. And he was clothed with a vesture dipped in blood: and his name is called The Word of God. And the armies which were in heaven followed him upon white horses, clothed in fine linen, white and clean. And out of his mouth goeth a sharp sword, that with it he should smite the nations: and he shall rule them with a rod of iron: and he treadeth the winepress of the fierceness and wrath of Almighty God. And he hath on his vesture and on his thigh a name written, KING OF KINGS, AND LORD OF LORDS. And I saw an angel standing in the sun; and he cried with a loud voice, saying to all the fowls that fly in the midst of heaven, Come and gather yourselves together unto the supper of the great God
>
> —REVELATION 19:9, 11–17, KJV

166

The wedding supper of the Lamb has been preached about, sung about and dramatized throughout history as our hearts and imaginations strain to comprehend its grandeur. The glory that awaits us at the coming of Christ will only fully be revealed at that time. Yet our hope can be raised and our resolve to be a partaker of His glory strengthened just by reading these passages of Scripture that allow us to glimpse into the glory of God revealed in the heavens. As we meditate on them, the Holy Spirit can fill our hearts with expectancy and resolve to be a partaker of the glory that is to be revealed.

Rehearsing the revelations found in Scripture concerning the Second Coming of Christ, heaven, the New Jerusalem, heavenly streets of gold, angelic beings and divine worship can fill our hearts with expectancy and joy of what awaits us as God's glory is revealed. We need to allow the Holy Spirit to thrill our hearts with a vision of this glory that is to come. How far short do our goals and expectations fall from the goal of this victorious Christ who is described by John? Where is the focus of our life? The source of our power? We can be transformed into the image of Christ as we behold Him and allow ourselves to become bearers of His glory now. (See 2 Corinthians 3:18.) We can barely imagine who we will become when the kingdom of God is fully manifest in all its glory.

In Jesus' high priestly prayer, He asked the Father to glorify Him with the glory He had with Him before the world was (John 17:5). Then He continued to pray for His disciples and all who would follow after them: "Father, I desire that they also whom You gave Me may be with Me where I am, that they may behold My glory which You have given Me; for You loved Me before the foundation of the world" (v. 24). What

167

does He mean when He asks that we should be with Him where He is? He declares that He lived in glory with the Father before the world was and that He wants us to be there with Him. We need to ask the Holy Spirit to enlarge our capacity to receive the answer to Jesus' prayer so that He can place us in that glory that is to be revealed.

Jesus taught His disciples to pray: "Our Father which art in heaven, Hallowed be thy name. Thy kingdom come. Thy will be done in earth, as it is in heaven. Give us this day our daily bread. And forgive us our debts, as we forgive our debtors. And lead us not into temptation, but deliver us from evil: For thine is the *kingdom,* and the *power,* and the *glory, forever.* Amen" (Matt. 6:9–13, KJV, EMPHASIS ADDED).

His kingdom, His power and His glory are eternal realities that we must embrace if we are to become bearers of His glory. As believers, we are to pray the reality of this model prayer daily, asking for the kingdom of God to come and for the will of God to be done in earth. We must believe that this eternal kingdom of God will be revealed to us and in us and through us—that we can experience His kingdom, His power, and His glory—*forever!*

Notes

Chapter 1
What Is the Glory?

1. John Rea, *The Holy Spirit in the Bible,* (Lake Mary, FL: Creation House, 1990), 21.
2. Fuchsia Pickett, *Presenting the Holy Spirit,* Vol. 1 (Lake Mary, FL: Creation House, 1997), 61–80.
3. Ibid., 37–59.

Chapter 3
The Glory of God in Creation

1. Pickett, *Presenting the Holy Spirit.*
2. Fuchsia Pickett, *The Next Move of God* (Lake Mary, FL: Creation House, 1994), 16.

Chapter 4
Glory in Heavenly Creatures

1. Merrill F. Unger, *The New Unger's Bible Dictionary,* 2nd ed. (Chicago: Moody Press, 1988), s.v. "biblical demonology."
2. Ibid.
3. *International Standard Bible Encyclopaedia,* Electronic Database (Biblesoft, 1996).
4. Fuchsia Pickett, *Worship Him,* (Lake Mary, FL, Creation House, 2000), 162–163.

CHAPTER 5
THE GLORY REVEALED IN PATRIARCHS

1. "Exodus," *Matthew Henry Commentary* (New York: Fleming H. Revell), 328.
2. Kevin J. Connor, *The Tabernacle of David* (Portland, OR: The Center Press, 1976), 20.

CHAPTER 6
THE GLORY REVEALED IN WORSHIP

1. Conner, *The Tabernacle of David*, 80.
2. Ibid.
3. Ibid.
4. Ibid., 82–84.

CHAPTER 7
THE GLORY INCARNATE

1. Unger, *The New Unger's Bible Dictionary*, s.v. "incarnation."
2. Ibid.
3. Fuchsia Pickett, *The Prophetic Romance* (Lake Mary, FL: Creation House, 1996), 68–72.
4. *Nelson's Illustrated Bible Dictionary* (Nashville, TN: Thomas Nelson, 1986), s.v. "incarnation."
5. Ibid.
6. G. Campbell Morgan, *The Gospel According to John* (New York: Fleming H. Revell Co., 1943).
7. Abraham Kuyper, *The Work of the Holy Spirit* (Grand Rapids, MI: Wm. Eerdmans Publication Co.).

8. For a more complete discussion see Fuchsia Pickett, *Presenting the Holy Spirit,* vol. 2 (Lake Mary, FL: Creation House, 1998).

CHAPTER 8
GLORY IN TEMPLES OF CLAY

1. Fuchsia Pickett, *God's Dream* (Shippensburg, PA: Destiny Image, 1991).
2. Pickett, *God's Dream,* 70.
3. Pickett, *God's Dream.*

CHAPTER 9
GLORY IN THE CHURCH

1. Pickett, *The Next Move of God.*

Spirit Led Woman

EMPOWERED FOR PURPOSE

1-800-829-9133 • www.spiritledwoman.com

P.O. Box 420234 • Palm Coast, FL 32142-0234

---

www.spiritledwoman.com

Spirit Led Woman

EMPOWERED FOR PURPOSE